FUN FACTS ABOUT THE BIBLE YOU NEVER KNEW

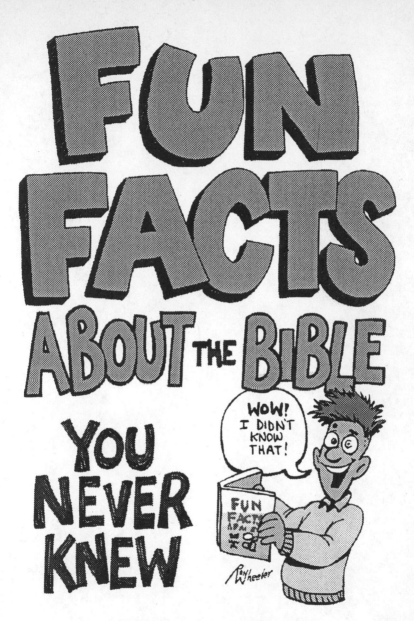

ROBYN MARTINS

A Barbour Book

Cover illustration: Ron Wheeler

Published by Barbour & Company, Inc.
P.O. Box 719
Uhrichsville, Ohio 44683
e-mail: books<barbour@tuso.net>

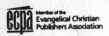 Member of the
Evangelical Christian
Publishers Association

Printed in the United States of America.

Let's Get Trivial!

Solomon had 700 wives and 300 concubines. Anniversaries must have been a problem.

The name Abraham (and Abram) is mentioned in the Bible 188 times. Sarah is only mentioned 31 times.

Adam was 130 years old when Seth was born. Genesis 5:3

Bethlehem means "house of bread."

Dodo was a descendant of Issachar. Who was Issachar? Why, the fifth son of Jacob and Leah, one of the 12 tribes of Israel. Judges 10:1, Genesis 30:17-18

Every three years Solomon's trading ships returned home with gold, silver, ivory, and a bunch of apes and baboons. Go figure. 1 Kings 10:22

Eliud was Jesus' great-great-great-grandfather.
Matthew 1:15

ARKTIFACTS AND MORE

Noah was a healthy 600 years old when God sent the flood. Genesis 7:6

A cubit is 18 inches long. That means the ark was 5400 inches long and 900 inches wide. Genesis 6:15

The ark was made of cypress wood (gopher wood in the King James Version). Genesis 6:14

Noah died at 950 years of age. Genesis 9:29

• • • • • • • • • • • • •

Jacob and Rachel were cousins. Genesis 29:10

In the entire book of Esther, God is not mentioned once.

Job's first daughter of his second family was named Jemimah. Job 42:14

An omer is equivalent to 2 quarts.

Israelites were forbidden to wear clothes made of two kinds of material. So much for 50% cotton/50% polyester. Leviticus 19:19

When the Arameans were camped outside Samaria, God made the sound of chariots and horses and a big army to scare them away. It worked. 2 Kings 7:6-7

David's warriors could shoot arrows right and left handed. 1 Chronicles 12:2

Obed's grandma Naomi was his nurse when he was a baby. Ruth 4:6

●●●●●●●●●●●●●

When King Xerxes couldn't sleep,
he had people read the record of
his reign to him. Esther 6:1

●●●●●●●●●●●●●

Jews tried to stone Jesus at the temple. They failed, of course. John 8:59

After Saul killed himself, the Philistines cut off his head and hung it in a temple. 1 Chronicles 10:10

When the Ark was on its way back to Israel, God killed 70 men who got curious and looked inside it. 1 Samuel 6:19

Manna tasted like honey wafers. Exodus 16:31

In ancient Israel, men closed a deal by exchanging sandals. Ruth 4:7

The Levites had a mandatory retirement age of 50 years.
Numbers 8:25

During a famine in Samaria, a donkey's head sold for 80
shekels of silver. 2 Kings 6:25

Moses' brother and sister were mad because he married a
Cushite woman. Numbers 12:1

If a Hebrew person found a bird's nest full of birds, he
could take the babies but had to leave the mother bird
behind. Deuteronomy 22:7

Ham, Noah's son, built Nineveh. Genesis 10:11

After Moses was given the Ten Commandments, he wore a
veil over his face because he glowed. Exodus 34:33-35

When Lot and his daughters moved out of Zoar, they lived
in a cave. Genesis 19:30

When meat was being boiled for a sacrifice, the priest got to
stick a fork in the pot and keep whatever it brought up.
1 Samuel 2:13

Elijah outran Ahab's chariots from Carmel all the way to
Jezreel. 1 Kings 18:46

Quiz Time!

1. What is the shortest chapter in the Bible?

2. We all know about Shadrach, Meshach, and Abednego, but do you know their names before they were changed?

3. Who was chosen to replace Judas Iscariot after he you know what?

4. Who was turned down to fill Judas' place as disciple?

5. Who was Moses' father?

6. How old was Adam when he died?

7. What was Peter's name in Aramaic? And don't say "Rock."

8. Who was a "wild donkey of a man?"

9. Who did Jesus take with Him to the mountain where He was transfigured?

10. Who said, "Nazareth! Can anything good come from there?"

QUIZ ANSWERS

1. Psalm 117. It has two verses.

2. Hananiah, Mishael, and Azariah. Daniel 1:7

3. Matthias. Acts 1:23-26

4. Barsabbas a.k.a. Justus a.k.a. Joseph. Acts 1:23

5. Amram, with some dispute. Numbers 26:59.

6. 930 years old. Genesis 5:5

7. Cephas. John 1:42

8. Ishmael, Hagar's son. Genesis 16:12

9. Peter, James, and John. Matthew 17:1

10. Nathanael. John 1:46

 What was the name of Ruth's sister-in-law?
Don't even think about looking it up.

Orpah. Ruth 1:4

What's in a Name?

The many names given to Jesus are familiar to most who have read the Bible, unless the consonants have been removed. Add the missing consonants to the vowels below to reveal some of Jesus' names.

Example: IAUEL = Immanuel

1. AA and OEA

2. I and I A

3. OO EE

4. I A

5. I of I

6. A of O

7. AE

8. IE of IE

9. OO of EE

10. UE IE

• • • • • • • • • • • • •

While you're thinking this over, finish Isaiah 9:6: "And he will be called. . ._____ _____, _____ _____, _____ _____, _____ ___ _____."

ANSWERS

1. Alpha and Omega. Revelation 1:11

2. Bright and Morning Star. Revelation 22:16

3. Good Shepherd. John 10:14

4. I Am. John 8:58

5. King of Kings. Revelation 19:16

6. Lamb of God. John 1:29

7. Master. John 1:38

8. Prince of Life. Acts 3:15

9. Root of Jesse. Isaiah 11:10

10. True Vine. John 15:1

• • • • • • • • • • • •

*Isaiah 9:6: And he will be called
Wonderful Counselor, Mighty God,
Everlasting Father, Prince of Peace.*

Nine to Five

Demetrius was a silversmith. Acts 19:24

Paul was a tentmaker. Acts 18:1-3

Joseph, Mary's husband, was a carpenter. Matthew 13:15

Alexander was a metal worker. 2 Timothy 4:14

Luke was a medical doctor. Colossians 4:14

Lydia was a saleswoman. Acts 16:14

Zacchaeus was a tax collector. Luke 19:2

Tertullus was a lawyer. Acts 24:1

Odds and Omegas

Evidently, Amram and Jochebed didn't name their son. It was Pharaoh's daughter who called him Moses.
Exodus 2:10

Did you know that when Jesus died, saints rose from the dead and walked around Jerusalem? Matthew 27:52-53

There are a lot of "wolves in sheep's clothing" these days. But Jesus used the term to describe false prophets a couple thousand years ago. Matthew 7:15

The ultimate sarcasm: God described the people in Nineveh as not knowing their left from their right. Jonah 4:11

Ruth's first husband was Mahlon. Ruth 4:10

They had peanut butter in the Bible—Ezekiel's tongue was stuck to the roof of his mouth until the Lord gave him words. Ezekiel 3:26-27

Animals have to answer to God, too. Genesis 9:5

Paul was beaten five times and shipwrecked three.
2 Corinthians 11:24-25

Who Said. . .?

1. "Lord, why can't I follow you now? I lay down my life for you."

2. "Indeed, women have been kept from us. . ."

3. "You son of a perverse and rebellious woman!"

4. "From now on all generations will call me blessed."

5. "After I am worn out and my master is old, will I now have this pleasure?"

6. "Even up to half the kingdom, it will be given you."

7. "Look, your sister-in-law is going back to her people and her gods. Go back with her."

8. "...whatever comes out of the door of my house to meet me when I return in triumph from the Ammonites will be the Lord's, and I will sacrifice it as a burnt offering."

9. "...The joy of the Lord is your strength."

10. "What have I done to you to make you beat me these three times?"

THEY DID!

1. Peter. John 13:37

2. David. 1 Samuel 21:5

3. King Saul. 1 Samuel 20:30

4. Mary. Luke 1:48

5. Sarah. Genesis 18:12

6. King Xerxes. Esther 5:3; and Herod. Mark 6:23

7. Naomi. Ruth 1:15

8. Jephthah. Judges 11:30

9. Nehemiah. Nehemiah 8:10

10. Balaam's donkey. Numbers 22:28

? What did John the Baptist eat?

Locusts and wild honey. Matthew 3:4

A TRIVIAL WORDSEARCH

It isn't much fun playing with familiar names and places. Where's the challenge in finding a word like Judah or Bethlehem? So, here is a true challenge—20 cities mentioned here and there in the Old Testament. If you can find them all, give yourself a bowl of raspberry sherbet. If you can find them on a map, give yourself a roundtrip ticket to Ziklag.

```
B T E B H E S H B O N
G A R A A L U Z N A I
M B M M R T B O U L B
A E D O R O E E Z U L
T Z E T V L J H T A E
T I T H N A N J B A A
A K A L H D U M A H M
N L J A A Z A H I A R
A A R K R C H J K N A
H G A B A F O G B E C
B I Z E N N P F E S H
```

Abez	Luz	Dumah	Hanes
Ijon	Dor	Eltolad	Jebus
Mattanah	Hara	Ibleam	Ono
Heshbon	Bamoth	Jaazah	Etam
Gaba	Ithnan	Nezib	Ziklag

WORDSEARCH SOLUTION

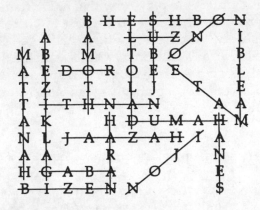

●●●●●●●●●●●●●

*The three magi were never **actually** at the traditional manger scene. They saw Jesus a little later at Joseph and Mary's house. Matthew 2:11*

FOR BETTER OR FOR WORSE
CLUE: WE'RE ALL MARRIED COUPLES

1. After we gave a little money to the apostles and put some more in our pockets, we fell on the floor, so to speak.

2. We moved from Italy to Corinth and made tents with Paul.

3. We traveled a lot and started our very own nation.

4. We first met in a grain field, cold feet and all.

5. Our first son died as a baby, but our second son was a royally smart guy.

6. We had three children with funny names, and after a short separation, rejoined at an auction block.

7. We ate quite often and were the end of that nasty Haman.

8. We ran for our lives at the warning of two angels, but one of us didn't quite make it.

9. We prayed to God for a son, and He gave us Samuel.

10. John the Baptist thought we shouldn't be married, so we snuffed him out.

THE HAPPY COUPLES

1. Ananias and Sapphira. Acts 5:1ff

2. Aquila and Priscilla. Acts 18:23

3. Abraham and Sarah. Genesis 12:1-2

4. Ruth and Boaz. Ruth 3:7-8

5. David and Bathsheba. 2 Samuel 12:5-24

6. Hosea and Gomer. Hosea 1-3

7. Esther and King Xerxes. Esther 5-7

8. Lot and his wife (name not given). Genesis 19

9. Elkanah and Hannah. 1 Samuel 1:2

10. Herod and Herodias. Matthew 14:3

• • • • • • • • • • • • •

The iron point alone on Goliath's spear weighed about 15 pounds. 1 Samuel 17:7

TRUE / FALSE

Pencils ready?

1. Abram traveled with his father away from his home in Uz.

2. God said to Noah, "Whoever sheds the blood of man, by man shall his blood be shed..."

3. Peter baptized Lydia in Philippi.

4. Isaac told people that his wife was his sister to save his skin.

5. Joseph was 23 when his brothers sold him to the Ishmaelites.

6. Jesus fed 4000 people with a few loaves of bread and some fish.

7. Moses and Abraham appeared with Jesus on the Mount of Transfiguration.

8. Samson was a judge over Israel for 20 years.

9. The clothes of John the Baptist were made of goat skin.

10. Lazarus had been in his tomb for three days when Jesus called him out.

T/F Answers

1. False. Abram was from Ur, not Uz. Genesis 11:31

2. True. Genesis 9:6

3. False. Paul baptized Lydia. Acts 16:15

4. True. So did his father Abraham. Genesis 26:7

5. False. He was 17. Genesis 37:2

6. True. Even though most people only talk about the 5000 people, this is still amazing. Matthew 15:29-39

7. False. Moses and Elijah appeared with him. Matthew 17:3

8. True. Judges 16:31

9. Get real. They were made of camel's hair. Matthew 3:4

10. False. He was in his tomb for four days. Remember, Martha was afraid he would smell. John 11:39

• • • • • • • • • • • • •

Herod was struck down by God, and his body was eaten by worms. Acts 13:23

ZANY MISCELLANY

Jair, a judge of Israel, had 30 sons who rode 30 donkeys, and controlled 30 towns.   Judges 10:3-4

and

Ibzan, a judge, had 30 sons and 30 daughters. Judges 12:9

and

Abdon, another judge, had 40 sons and 30 grandsons who rode on 70 donkeys. Judges 12:14

The familiar story of Jesus saying, "If any one of you is without sin, let him be the first to throw a stone at her" (John 7:53-8:11) is found nowhere else in the Bible. In fact, it isn't even found in many manuscripts of the Gospels.

Abraham's father was named Terah. Genesis 11:26

The term "scapegoat" comes from the use of a goat that was to receive the sins of the people and be released into the wilderness. Leviticus 16:10

Thomas, the one who is always ridiculed for skepticism, is also known as Didymus. John 20:24

You may have heard people exclaim, "Jehoshaphat!" Well, Jehoshaphat is the valley where God will judge the nations according to Joel 3:2. It's also the name of the fourth king of Judah.

Jezebel was so bad that she had Naboth stoned to death just to get his vineyard. 1 Kings 21:1-16

Moses was four months old when Pharaoh's daughter found him in the basket. Acts 7:20-21

When Paul was in a shipwreck off the shore of Malta, there were 276 people on board. Acts 27:37

• • • • • • • • • • • •

Nahor, Abraham's grandfather, means "snorer."

• • • • • • • • • • • •

When Lazarus came out of the grave, only his hands, feet, and face were wrapped with cloth. John 11:44

When Elizabeth was pregnant with John the Baptist, Zecharias was struck dumb until the baby was born. Luke 1

Moses had two wives, Zipporah and a Cushite woman. Exodus 2:21 and Numbers 12:1

EMBATTLED HYMNS

Decipher these Scripture excerpts to find inspirations for
some of our favorite hymns.

1. . . .BUEV,BUEV, BUEV, EUSA PUA CEFDPBNZ.

2. . . .XTAMS BDH IDTPH VUX IDEE MDTA SJMXPJ.

3. D QTUI NBCN FV SJAJJFJS EDOJNB.

4. PEUSDUXH NBDTPH CSJ HWUQJT UM NBJJ. . .

ANSWERS

1. Holy, holy, holy, Lord God almighty. Revelation 4:8

2. Under his wings you will find refuge. Psalm 91:4

3. I know that my redeemer liveth. Job 19:25

4. Glorious things of thee are spoken. Psalm 87:3

? Of course, Jacob had 12 sons, but who was his only daughter?

Dinah, the one who was defiled by Shechem and caused such an uproar. Genesis 34:1

Elijah/Elisha

Elijah, Elisha, Elisha, Elijah. Which one was which? That's easy, but your job is to decide who did what. Fill in the blanks.

1. After he warned Ahab of a drought, _____ hid by a river and got food from birds, ravens to be exact.

2. Some prophets yelled, "There is death in the pot! Then, _____ put some flour in the stew, and everything was O.K.

3. Twenty loaves of barley bread fed 100 people when _____ told a man to feed them.

4. Some kids called _____ a baldhead. So, he cursed them.

5. The widow at Zarephath had a son who stopped breathing, so _____ prayed and brought him back to life.

6. _____ made fun of the prophets of Asherah when they couldn't get Baal to start a fire.

7. Someone lost an axe head in the Jordan River. So, _____ made it float.

8. When _____ prayed, God made a whole band of enemy Arameans blind.

9. _____ gave a widow jar after jar of oil to pay her bills.

10. _____ was a Tishbite.

WHO'S WHO?

1. Elijah. 1 Kings 17:5

2. Elisha. 2 Kings 4:38-41

3. Elisha. 2 Kings 4:44

4. Elisha. 2 Kings 2:23

5. Elijah. 1 Kings 17:17-23

6. Elijah. 1 Kings 18:27

7. Elisha. 2 Kings 6:1-7

8. Elisha. 2 Kings 6:18

9. Elisha. 2 Kings 4:1-7

10. Elijah. 1 Kings 17:1

WAR AND PIECES

Joseph's tribe was split in two. His sons Ephraim and Manasseh got their own land allotments. Joshua 16:4

With Nehemiah as the foreman, it took 52 days to rebuild Jerusalem's wall. Nehemiah 6:15

Stephen was the first recorded Christian martyr. He was stoned to death. Acts 7:59-60

• • • • • • • • • • •

Israelites weren't allowed to eat camels.
What a sacrifice! Well, actually, they
couldn't sacrifice them either.
Leviticus 11:4

• • • • • • • • • • •

When Joshua's army was taking over parts of Canaan, they crippled their enemy's horses by clipping their hamstrings. Joshua 11:9

When Saul couldn't get his armor-bearer to kill him, he committed suicide by falling on his own sword.
1 Samuel 31:4

Antipas was a martyr who lived in Pergamum, one of the Asian cities named in Revelation. Revelation 2:13

When Pharaoh gave orders to kill all Hebrew baby boys, Shiphrah and Puah, two Hebrew midwives, refused to do it. Exodus 1:15

When God finally spoke to Job, he spoke from out of a storm. Job 38: 1, 40:6

Joshua made the Gibeonites be woodcutters and water carriers for the Israelites as a curse. Joshua 9:23

Joseph, Mary, and Jesus moved to Egypt for awhile because Herod wanted to kill Jesus. Matthew 2:13

Esau's third wife, Mahalath, was also his cousin Ishmael's daughter. Genesis 28:9

? Jonah wasn't the only one sent to Nineveh. What other prophet ministered there?

Nahum. Nahum 1:1

Moses had two sons, Gershom and Eliezer. Exodus 18:3

Samson set the tails of 300 foxes on fire and set the poor animals loose in some Philistine grain fields.
Judges 15:4-5

In Old Testament times people wore sackcloth so other people would know they were in mourning. 2 Samuel 3:31

WHERE DO YOU FIND IT, ANYWAY?

Below are some familiar Bible passages that people often like to quote. They aren't necessarily trivial, but their references aren't as easily recognized. So, where do you find them, anyway?

1. Jesus wept.

2. There is no one righteous, not even one.

3. They will soar on wings like eagles; they will run and not grow weary, they will walk and not be faint.

4. The Lord is my shepherd, I shall not be in want.

5. For the wages of sin is death, but the gift of God is eternal life in Christ Jesus our Lord.

6. A man reaps what he sows.

7. Glory to God in the highest, and on earth peace to men on whom his favor rests.

8. There is a time for everything, and a season for every activity under heaven.

9. Let my people go, so that they may worship me.

10. This cup is the new covenant in my blood, which is poured out for you.

OPEN YOUR BIBLES

1. John 11:35

2. Romans 13:10

3. Isaiah 40:31b

4. Too easy! Psalm 23:1

5. Romans 6:23

6. Galatians 6:7

7. Luke 2:14

8. Ecclesiastes 3:1

9. Exodus 8:1

10. Luke 22:20

• • • • • • • • • • • • •

*Locusts, katydids, crickets, and grasshoppers
were considered clean food for the Israelites.
What's for lunch? Leviticus 11:22*

QUIZ TIME!

1. What was Achan's sin?

2. Why did Paul shave his head?

3. What evangelist had four daughters who prophesied?

4. James and John were the sons of Zebedee, but who was their mother?

5. Who put Jesus in the tomb?

6. What was the Ethiopian eunuch reading when he met Philip?

7. What was the answer to Samson's riddle, "Out of the eater, something to eat; out of the strong, something sweet."

8. When Jesus wept, why did he weep, or what was the occasion?

9. Moses made a bronze snake. For what was it an antidote?

10. Methuselah lived longer than anyone else recorded in the Bible. Who came in second?

QUIZ ANSWERS

1. He took some devoted things from Jericho. Joshua 7:1

2. It marked the end of a vow he had taken. Acts 18:18

3. Philip. Acts 21:8-9

4. Salome. Mark 15:40

5. Joseph of Arimathea and Nicodemus. John 19:38-39

6. The Book of Isaiah. Acts 8:28

7. Honey from a lion's carcass. Judges 14:14

8. The lack of faith of his followers, or Lazarus' death. John 11:35

9. The bite of venomous snakes. Numbers 21:4-9

10. Jared, Methuselah's grandfather. Genesis 5:20

ESOTERIC RHETORIC

King Jehoshaphat built a fleet of trading ships that were wrecked before they ever set sail. 1 Kings 22:48

When Nineveh repented, its residents even put sackcloth on all their animals. Jonah 3:8

Meshech, the grandson of Shem, was also known as Mash (Hebrew). Wouldn't you use a different name, too? 1 Chronicles 1:17

Job had 3000 camels, at first. Job 1:3

Whole books are dedicated to the escapades of the kings of Israel and Judah. But did you know that Judah once had a ruling queen? Queen Athaliah ruled for six years. 2 Kings 11:3

Mordecai acted as Esther's father, but he was really her cousin. Esther 2:7

Isaiah wrote with an ordinary pen, as opposed to an unusual one. Isaiah 8:1

The Israelites called their communities together by blowing two silver trumpets. Numbers 10:23

HOT STUFF
(OR HOW FIRE WAS USED IN THE OLD TESTAMENT)

The burning bush was obviously on fire. Exodus 3:2

A pillar of fire led Israel at night. Exodus 13:21

Elijah was taken by a chariot and horses of fire. 2 Kings 2:11

Sodom and Gomorrah were destroyed by fire.
Genesis 19:24

The Lord descended on Mt. Sinai with fire. Exodus 19:18

Twice, "fire from Heaven" consumed a captain and 50 men
who were a threat to Elijah. 2 Kings 1:9-12

Fire consumed the outskirts of the camp when the Israelites
wouldn't stop whining. Numbers 11:11

"Fire of God" destroyed Job's sheep and servants. Job 1:16

Fire killed 250 men after they opposed Moses and Aaron.
Numbers 16:35

THE PLAGUES

(OR, HOW REAL ESTATE PLUMMETED IN EGYPT)

Name the plagues God sent to Egypt to convince them to "Let my people go!" They must be in order to get full credit.

1.

2.

3.

4.

5.

7.

8.

9.

10.

THE PLAGUES IN ORDER
(EXODUS 7:14 TO CHAPTER 11)

1. The Nile was turned into blood.

2. Frogs came from water.

3. Dust was turned into gnats.

4. Flies were everywhere.

5. All the livestock died.

6. Everybody had boils.

7. Hail destroyed the crops.

8. Locusts ate what the hail missed.

9. There were three straight days of darkness.

10. The first born son of every family died.

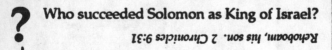

? **Who succeeded Solomon as King of Israel?**

Rehoboam, his son. 2 Chronicles 9:31

AND GOD SAID. . .

To whom did God say the following:

1. I will make your offspring like the dust of the earth, so that if anyone could count the dust, then your offspring could be counted.

2. Two nations are in your womb, and two peoples from within you will be separated.

3. Your house and your kingdom will endure forever before me; your throne will be established forever.

4. I will heal you . . . I will add 15 years to your life.

5. Whom shall I send? And who will go for us?

6. Before I formed you in the womb I knew you, before you were born I set you apart.

7. There is no one on earth like him; he is blameless and upright, a man who fears God and shuns evil.

8. Let the water teem with living creatures, and let birds fly above the earth. . . .

9. Take off your sandals, for the place where you are standing is holy ground.

10. Go, take to yourself an adulterous wife and children of unfaithfulness. . . .

GOD SPOKE TO. . .

1. Abram. Genesis 13:16

2. Rebekah. Genesis 25:23a

3. David. 2 Samuel 7:16-17

4. Hezekiah via Isaiah. 2 Kings 20:5-6

5. Isaiah. Isaiah 6:8

6. Jeremiah. Jeremiah 1:5

7. Satan about Job. Job 1:8

8. The earth. Genesis 1:20

9. Moses. Exodus 3:5

10. Hosea. 1:2

• • • • • • • • • • • •

Illyricum, a place Paul once mentioned, is
actually Albania and Yugoslavia.
Romans 15:19

WHAT DOES IT MEAN, ANYWAY?

Amen means "so let it be."

Selah? Nobody really knows, but it was probably a musical term. Psalm 3:2

An ephah is a dry measure of more than half a bushel. Ezekiel 45:10

Onycha is an expensive incense like musk that Moses used. Exodus 30:34

Goad or oxgoad: a wooden pole used to clean plows and prod animals. Judges 3:31

A handstaff is a staff in the hand. What did you think? Ezekiel 39:9 (KJV)

Crisping pins were purses. Isaiah 3:22

Nitre is a baking soda-type stuff used to make soap. Proverbs 25:20

A withe is a strong twig (a thong in the NIV). Judges 16:7-9

OFF THE RECORD

Shem, Noah's son, was the ancestor of the Jewish people. Genesis 11:10-26

Abraham's servant went all the way to Mesopotamia to find a wife for Isaac. Genesis 24:10

It didn't rain in the Garden of Eden, or out of it for that matter. Water came up from the ground to make things grow. Genesis 2:5-6

Gideon laid out the fleece looking for a sign from the Lord because he wanted to beat the Midianites in battle the next day. Judges 6:36-40

• • • • • • • • • • • • •

Job's wife thought he had bad breath. Job 19:17

• • • • • • • • • • • •

Solomon was called Solomon until the day he died, but when he was born, God named him Jedidiah. 2 Samuel 12:25

Daniel and his friends ate nothing but vegetables and water for ten days. Daniel 1:12

The Ammonites tried to embarrass David's men by shaving off half their beard and cutting off their clothes at about mid-buttocks length. It must have worked. 2 Samuel 10:4

AN ANIMAL WORDSEARCH

The Bible is full of animals. They were ridden, slaughtered, talked to, and even listened to. In Psalm 80 Asaph wrote about an animal who ravaged the "vine out of Egypt." What was it? Hint: It's hidden in the wordsearch twice.

```
C A M R G A B A T S E
O B O A R W E A S E L
R O R O E L H U L Y E
A A E Z Y K E O N E V
L R B C H A M O I S I
H O O P O E O R A E A
I A P N U L T H A R T
N S W I N E H P Z M H
D P L C D S A T Y R A
C B I P Y G A R G E N
Z E B O I M C O N E Y
```

Behemoth	Chamois	Coney
Greyhound	Hart	Leviathan
Mole	Pygarg	Roe
Satyr	Weasel	Asp
Coral	Swine	Hind
Zeboim	Boar	Bats

ANIMAL WORDSEARCH SOLUTION

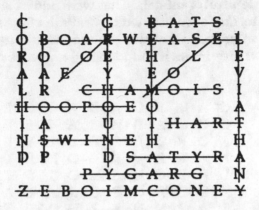

The animal that ravaged the "vine out of Egypt"
was a BOAR.

STAFF ONLY

And God said, "But take this STAFF in your hand
so you can perform miraculous signs with it."
Exodus 4:17

When Moses threw it on the ground it turned into a snake, and he ran away from it. Exodus 4:4

It turned into a snake again in front of Pharaoh.
Exodus 7:10

Most of the plagues in Egypt were brought on with the staff.

Moses divided the Red Sea with it. Exodus 14:16

Moses hit the rock of Horeb with it to get water.
Exodus 17:6

Aaron's staff budded and produced almonds.
Numbers 17:8

Moses hit a rock twice to get water, even though he was just supposed to talk to the thing. Numbers 25:11

HELP ME RHODA
(AND A FEW OTHER GOLDEN OLDIES)

Rhoda was the servant girl who answered the door when Peter escaped from jail. Acts 12:13

Phoebe was a deacon who was highly valued by Paul. She may have even delivered the letter to the Romans. Romans 16:1-2

Abigail saved her silly husband from David's wrath, and after the guy died, she married David. 1 Samuel 25

Anna was an 84-year-old prophet who praised God for the baby Jesus at the Temple in Jerusalem. Luke 2:36-38

Junias was an apostle who was once imprisoned with Paul. Romans 16:7

Huldah warned of impending judgment of Judah. 2 Kings 22:14

Joanna was one of the women who discovered that Jesus had risen and left the tomb. Luke 24:10

DISCIPLE MATCH-UP
AS LISTED IN LUKE 6:14-16

Match them up with their a.k.a.'s, relations, or otherwise brief descriptions.

1. Simon Peter

2. Andrew

3. James

4. John

5. Philip

6. Bartholomew

7. Matthew

8. Thomas

9. James the less

10. Simon (Zealot)

11. Judas

12. Judas Iscariot

a. Alphaeus' son

b. Also called Thaddaeus

c. Andrew's brother

d. A friend of Bartholomew's

e. Also called Levi

f. James' brother

g. Also called Didymus

h. Son of a Simon

i. Also called the Cananaen

j. Simon Peter's brother

k. John's brother

l. Also called Nathanael

Matched-up Disciples

1. c. Simon Peter and Andrew were brothers.

2. j. Ditto.

3. k. James and John were brothers.

4. f. Ditto.

5. d. Philip and Bartholomew were friends.

6. l. Bartholomew was also called Nathanael.

7. e. Matthew was also called Levi.

8. g. Thomas was also called Didymus.

9. a. James the less was Alphaeus' son.

10. i. Simon the Zealot was once called a Cananaen.

11. b. Judas was also called Thaddaeus.

12. h. Judas Iscariot was the son of a Simon. There are so many.

THE BACK FORTY
(WAY BACK WHEN!)

Jonah told Nineveh that in 40 days the city would be overturned. Jonah 3:4

Jesus fasted for 40 days in the desert. Matthew 4:2 says, "...he was hungry." Imagine that.

After the Resurrection, Jesus was on earth for 40 days. Acts 1:3

Moses was 40 years old when he first visited the Israelites in Egypt. Acts 7:23

He was another 40 years older when he saw the burning bush. Acts 7:30

And, he was another 40 years older when he died. Deuteronomy 34:7

Goliath challenged the Israelites twice a day for 40 days. 1 Samuel 17:16

While Deborah judged Israel, the people lived in peace for 40 years. Behind every peaceful country, there is a good woman. Judges 5:31

There were also 40 years of peace under Gideon's judgeship. Judges 8:38

DROUGHT, ANYONE?

The Israelites crossed the Red Sea on dry ground, of course. But this miracle was repeated a few more times on occasions that evidently don't rate a Hollywood effort.

The Israelites crossed the Jordan with the ark of the covenant. Joshua 4:7

Elijah divided the Jordan with his coat, of all things.
2 Kings 2:8

Elisha was left with Elijah's coat and used it to part the Jordan again. 2 Kings 2:14

The Lord will split the Euphrates into seven streams "so that men can cross in sandals" (Isaiah 11:15) or high-tops, depending on the times.

THE FULL ARMOR OF GOD

"Therefore put on the full armor of God, so that when the day of evil comes, you may be able to stand your ground. . . ." Ephesians 6:13

Fill in the blanks:

1. Belt of _____.

2. Breastplate of _____.

3. Feet fitted with _____.

4. Shield of _____.

5. Helmet of _____.

6. Sword of _____.

ANSWERS

1. Belt of TRUTH.

2. Breastplate of RIGHTEOUSNESS.

3. Feet fitted with READINESS.

4. Shield of FAITH.

5. Helmet of SALVATION.

6. Sword of THE SPIRIT.

•••••••••••••

*The disciples were first called Christians
in Antioch. Acts 11:26*

FACTS IT TO ME

The covering for the tabernacle was made out of ram skins and sea cow hides. Exodus 36:19

Joseph's brothers didn't sell him directly to the Egyptians. They sold him to some Midianites who sold him to Potiphar in Egypt. Genesis 38:36

When Elisha learned that Jericho had bad water, he made it better by tossing in about a bowl full of salt water. 2 Kings 2:21

• • • • • • • • • •

People weren't given permission to eat meat until after the Flood. Genesis 9:3

• • • • • • • • • •

The Gospel of Luke and the book of Acts were both written to somebody named Theophilus.

Once Ezekiel was sitting in his house when a big hand picked him up by the hair of his head and took him somewhere between heaven and earth. Ezekiel 8:3

For years the Israelites burned incense to the bronze snake that Moses made, until Hezekiah broke it up. 2 Kings 18:4

King Saul's wife was named Ahinoam. 1 Samuel 14:50

First Things First

Cain built the first city. 4:17

Jubal was the father of people who play harps and flutes. 4:21

Cain committed the first murder. 4:8

Noah planted the first vineyard. 9:20

Lamech was the first polygamist. 4:19

Abel was the first shepherd. 4:2

Cain was the first farmer. 4:2

Tubal-cain was the first iron worker. Did he start the union, too? 4:22

Abram was the first Hebrew. 13:14

ALL SHOOK UP

Rearrange the "all shook up" letters below to spell some of the kings. Then decide whether they ruled Israel or Judah.

1. MHOBOARE

2. SABAAH

3. SHPHTHJEOAA

4. HHEOAJAZ

5. AAAMIZH

6. SMALULH

7. KAHAHIEP

8. SHAIJO

9. LAATHIHA

10. DEEKIHAZ

ANSWERS

1. King Rehoboam of Judah

2. King Baasha of Israel

3. King Jehoshaphat of Judah

4. King Jehoahaz of Israel

5. King Amaziah of Judah

6. King Shallum of Israel

7. King Pekahiah of Israel

8. King Josiah of Judah

9. Queen Athaliah of Judah

10. King Zedekiah of Judah

• • • • • • • • • • •

*King Ahab disguised himself in a battle
so the enemy wouldn't try to kill him, but a random
arrow hit him anyway. 1 Kings 22:29-35*

BLIND SPOTS

"Apple of your eye" is hardly a new expression. Solomon said it in Proverbs 7:2.

The Sabbath was measured from the evening of one day to the evening of the next. Leviticus 23:32

When Stephen spoke to the Sanhedrin, he gave a history lesson from Abraham all the way to Solomon. It was the first recorded filibuster. Acts 7:1-47

? "An eye for an eye" was an Old Testament rule of thumb. What was Jesus' rule for responding to an offense?

Turn the other cheek. Matthew 5:38-39

Haman had a gallows built to hang Mordecai, but he was hanged on it instead. Esther 7:9

Here's a phrase that has stood the test of time—Job was the first recorded person to say "the skin of my teeth." Job 19:20

When Moses led the Israelites out of Egypt, he took Joseph's bones. Exodus 13:19

John was on the island of Patmos when he wrote Revelation. Revelation 1:9

Third Time's the Charm

Jonah was inside the big fish for three days. Jonah 1:17

Peter denied Christ three times. Matthew 26:34

Jesus rose after three days. John 2:19

Paul was blind for three days. Acts 9:9

Esther fasted for three days before she spoke to the King.
Esther 4:16

Isaiah went around stripped and barefoot for three years as
a sign against Egypt. Isaiah 20:3

Elijah stretched himself out over a widow's son three times
to bring him back to life. 1 Kings 17:21

POP QUIZ

Name the fathers of all these people.

1. Seth.

2. Isaiah.

3. Ham.

4. Boaz.

5. Joseph (Mary's husband).

6. Jonah.

7. Samson.

8. Noah.

9. Lot.

10. Sarah.

Answers

1. Adam begat Seth. Genesis 4:25

2. Amoz begat Isaiah. Isaiah 1:1

3. Noah begat Ham. Genesis 5:32

4. Salmon begat Boaz. Matthew 1:5

5. Jacob begat Joseph, Mary's husband. Matthew 1:16

6. Amittai begat Jonah. Jonah 1:1

7. Manoah begat Samson. Judges 13:2

8. Lamech begat Noah. Genesis 5:29

9. Haran begat Lot. Genesis 11:27

10. Terah begat Sarah. Genesis 20:12

TRUE / FALSE

1. In Pharaoh's dream seven gaunt cows ate seven sleek cows.

2. King Herod gave the head of John the Baptist to his wicked wife.

3. King Belshazzar had Daniel tossed in the lions' den.

4. Solomon was made king before David died.

5. Jesus was 33 years old when He started His ministry.

6. Noah's son Japheth was older than his brother Shem.

7. After Jesus left the tomb, the first person who saw Him was John.

8. It took Elisha just one try to set fire to his drenched sacrifice.

9. Aaron died on Mount Hor, after he gave his clothes to his son.

10. Elisha saw Elijah take off from west of the Jordan River.

ANSWERS

1. True. Genesis 41:4

2. False. He gave it to his stepdaughter. Matthew 14:6-11

3. False. It was King Darius. Daniel 6

4. True. 1 Kings 1:43

5. False. He was about 30 years old. Luke 3:23

6. True. Genesis 10:21

7. False. Mary Magdalene saw him first. Mark 16:9

8. False. It was Elijah who prayed for fire to burn the bull.
   1 Kings 18:36-37

9. True. Numbers 20:28

10. False. They were on the east side. 2 Kings 2:8

? Who did Pontius Pilate release to the Jews
instead of Jesus?

Barabbas, a murderer. Mark 15:15

KING ME!

(CHECK(ER) IT OUT)

Solomon's traders imported horses and chariots from Egypt. 2 Chronicles 1:17

Eglon, king of Moab, was so fat that when Ehud stabbed him with a one and a half foot long sword, the handle sank into his belly. Judges 3:22

Esther's Hebrew name was Hadassah. Esther 2:7

When Paul and Barnabas were speaking in Lystra, they were mistaken for the gods Hermes and Zeus by people in the crowd. Acts 14:12

? What were the names of Job's three "friends?"

Eliphaz, Bildad, and Zophar. Job 2:11

Jacob changed his youngest son's name from Ben-oni, chosen by Rachel, to Benjamin. Genesis 35:18

When Abraham told people that Sarah was his sister, he was only half lying. They had the same father. Genesis 20:12

When David crept up behind Saul and cut off a corner of his robe, did you know that Saul was actually relieving himself? 1 Samuel 24:3-4

When Paul was building a fire, a poisonous snake bit him on the hand. People thought he was a god when he didn't die. Acts 28:1-6

Jerusalem was once called Jebus. Judges 19:10

The Sea of Galilee was also known as the Sea of Tiberias. John 21:1

Timothy was raised by his grandmother, Lois, and his mother, Eunice. 2 Timothy 1:5

Solomon had 12,000 horses. 1 Kings 10:26

? What are the four rivers in the Garden of Eden?

Pishon, Gihon, Tigris, and Euphrates. Genesis 2:11-14

Do you remember the Midianite woman and the Israelite man that Phinehas killed with a stake? They were Cozbi, daughter of Zur, and Zimri, son of Salu, respectively. Numbers 25:14-15

Isaac was 40 years old when he married Rebekah. Genesis 25:20

Jericho was the City of Palms. Judges 1:16

J - WALK

Fill in the blanks to complete the words that are described. Obviously, they all start with the letter J.

1. J__ __ __ __ __. A river east of the Jordan where Jacob met an angel.

2. J__ __ __ __ __ __ __. A famous son of King Saul.

3. J__ __ __ __ __ __-J__ __ __ __. Abraham almost sacrificed Isaac there.

4. J__ __ __ __ __ __ __. An Israelite judge who sacrificed his daughter.

5. J__ __ __ __ __ __. A city with a lot of history, it fell down after a week-long siege.

6. J__ __ __ __ __ __. Jezebel was eaten by dogs in this city.

7. J__ __ __ __ __ __ __. She put her baby in a basket to save his life.

8. J__ __ __ __ __ __ __. A prophet under Josiah, king of Judah.

9. J__ __ __. A prophet whose name meant "The Lord is God."

10. J__ __ __ __. The father of Bukki. Hint: See Numbers 34:22.

J Names

1. Jabbok. Genesis 32:22-30

2. Jonathan. 1 Samuel 13:16

3. Jehovah-Jireh. Genesis 22:14

4. Jephthah. Judges 11:39

5. Jericho. Joshua 6:20

6. Jezreel. 2 Kings 9:36

7. Jochebed. Exodus 2:3

8. Jeremiah. Jeremiah 1:1-2

9. Joel. Joel 1:1

10. Jogli. Numbers 34:22

The Beatitudes
Matthew 5:3-10

These words are anything but trivial, but blessed are you if you can complete each phrase.

1. Blessed are the poor in spirit,. . . .

2. Blessed are those who mourn,. . . .

3. Blessed are the meek,. . . .

4. Blessed are those who hunger and thirst for righteousness,. . . .

5. Blessed are the merciful,. . . .

6. Blessed are the pure in heart,. . . .

7. Blessed are the peacemakers,. . . .

8. Blessed are those who are persecuted because of righteousness,. . . .

THE REST OF THE BEATITUDES

1. . . .for theirs is the kingdom of heaven.

2. . . .for they will be comforted.

3. . . .for they will inherit the earth.

4. . . .for they will be filled.

5. . . .for they will be shown mercy.

6. . . .for they will see God.

7. . . .for they will be called sons of God.

8. . . .for theirs is the kingdom of heaven.

? Where was Jonah trying to go when he ran away from his responsibilities in Nineveh?

Tarshish. Jonah 1:3

TRY TO REMEMBER

When the Israelites needed to relieve themselves, they had to go outside the camp and dig a hole.
Deuteronomy 23:12-13

The Exodus probably took place in 1446 B.C.

Psalm 119 is the longest chapter in the Bible with 176 verses.

Abraham had two nephews named Uz and Buz.
Genesis 22:21

Peter paid taxes for Jesus and himself with money he found in a fish's mouth. Not so trivial, but pretty strange.
Matthew 17:27

Everybody always says "Jesus fed five thousand," but that didn't include women and children. How about "Jesus fed the whole bunch." Matthew 14:21

The Philistine rulers each offered Delilah 1100 shekels of silver for telling them the secret of Samson's strength.
Judges 16:5

After the Resurrection, when Jesus told the disciples to put their fishing nets on the right side of the boat, they caught 153 fish. John 21:11

Forty Carats

The Flood, of course. Water flooded the earth for 40 days. Genesis 7:17

Moses was on Mount Sinai 40 days receiving instructions from God. Exodus 24:18

For some reason, it took 40 days to embalm a person back when Jacob was alive, or actually when Jacob was dead. Genesis 50:3

The Israelites ate manna for 40 years until they finally settled in Canaan. Exodus 16:35

The representatives of each Israelite tribe explored Canaan for 40 days before returning with their report to Moses. Numbers 13:25

After the Israelites put the nix on conquering Canaan, they were forced to wander in the desert for 40 years. Numbers 32:13

Saul, David, Solomon, and Joash all reigned as kings for 40 years.

Elijah traveled for 40 days until he reached Horeb. 1 Kings 19:8

PROPHETS SHMOPHETS

1. This prophet asked if a leopard could change his spots.

2. This one saw a flying scroll in a vision.

3. Who talks about the "sword of the Lord?"

4. This prophet ate a scroll. Hopefully, it was just a vision.

5. A seraph touched this prophet's mouth with a hot coal.

6. He made an axe head float in water.

7. Who was slapped in the face for calling one of King Ahab's prophets a liar?

8. This prophet wrote the shortest book of the Old Testament.

9. This one lost his shade tree to a hungry worm.

10. He was a shepherd and a fig-tree gardener.

ANSWERS

1. Jeremiah. Jeremiah 13:23

2. Zechariah saw a scroll 30 feet long and 15 feet wide. Zechariah 5:1-3

3. Isaiah. Isaiah 34:6

4. Ezekiel had the tasty treat. Ezekiel 3:3

5. Isaiah again. Isaiah 6:6-7

6. Elisha. 2 Kings 6:6

7. Micaiah was slapped. 1 Kings 22:24

8. Obadiah. Obadiah (all 21 verses)

9. Jonah. Jonah 4:6-8

10. Amos. Amos 7:14

? According to Solomon's proverb, what is in Wisdom's right and left hands?

Long life is in the right and riches and honor are in the left. Proverbs 3:16

Who Am I?

Fill in the blanks and unscramble the letters found in parentheses. The Gospel of Luke was written to this person.

1. I am the grandfather of Moab and Ben-Ammi. Come to think of it, I'm the father, too. _ _ (_)

2. My husband didn't love me very much. Was it because my eyes were weak? _ (_) _ (_)

3. I ate at David's table, and I was crippled in both feet. _ _ (_) _ _ _ (_) _ _ _ _ _

4. I visited Solomon and gave him all kinds of presents. What a guy! _ _ _ _ _   _ _   _ (_) _ _ _

5. King David gave me everything that belonged to Mephibosheth who had betrayed him. _ _ _ _

6. As king of Judah, I ousted my grandmother from the throne because she made a pagan idol. _ _ _

7. Some eunuchs threw me from my window, and dogs just ate me up. _ _ _ _ _ (_)

8. I was a "wee little man" in Jericho. _ _ _ _ _ _ (_) _

9. I traveled with Paul after his little tiff with Barnabas. _ (_) _ _

10. Paul left me with those Cretans who are "always liars, evil brutes, lazy gluttons." _ _ _ (_)

THE WHO

1. Lot. Genesis 19:36-38

2. Leah. Genesis 29:16

3. Mephibosheth. 2 Samuel 9

4. The Queen of Sheba. 1 Kings 10:1-13

5. Ziba. 2 Samuel 16:4

6. Asa. 1 Kings 5:13

7. Jezebel. 2 Kings 9:33-37

8. Zacchaeus. Luke 19:1-3

9. Silas. Acts 15:40

10. Titus. Titus 1:12

The Gospel of Luke was written to
THEOPHILUS.

Just The Facts, Ma'am

Before an Israelite could offer a ram as a burnt offering, he had to wash its legs with water. Leviticus 1:9

When Joseph found out that Mary was pregnant, he wanted to divorce her quietly. Even though they were only engaged, that was the proper way to be dismissed from the obligation. Matthew 2:19

Joash was a mere seven years old when he became king. 2 Chronicles 24:1

? What is another name for Lake of Gennesaret?

The Sea of Galilee. Luke 5:1

Og, the king of Bashan, had an iron bed 13 feet long and 6 feet wide. Deuteronomy 3:11

Nazareth to Bethlehem is approximately 70 miles as the crow flies. As the donkey trots, it's about a three day trip.

Shallum was a ruler of Israel for only one month before he was assassinated by his successor. 2 Kings 15:13

It took Solomon 13 years to build his palace. It only took him seven years to build the temple. 1 Kings 6:38-7:1

Camp Rules
(at least for the Israelites)

If you knock out your slave's tooth, you have to set him free. Exodus 21:27

If you don't confine your ox that is known for killing people, and your ox kills somebody, you and your ox have to die. This is the final warning. Exodus 21:29

No eating tendons attached to the hip of an animal. Refer to your camp rule book about what happened to Jacob. Genesis 32:24ff.

Do not charge interest to a fellow camper. Only charge interest to foreigners. Deuteronomy 23:20

No tattoos. Leviticus 20:28

No tripping blind people. Leviticus 19:14

Please pick up all donkeys and oxen found lying in the road. Let's keep our camp clean. Deuteronomy 22:3

Don't eat things with wings. Leviticus 11:23

FOLLOW ME
MULTIPLE CHOICE

1. Jesus first found him fishing in the Sea of Galilee.
   a. Matthew   b. Andrew   c. Judas

2. He and his brother left their father to follow Jesus.
   a. Andrew   b. James   c. Thomas

3. Jesus healed his mother-in-law.
   a. Matthew   b. James   c. Peter

4. Jesus called him away from his job at the tax collector's booth.
   a. Matthew   b. Philip   c. James

5. He tried to walk with Jesus on the water.
   a. Bartholomew   b. Peter   c. John

6. This one gave Jesus a kiss but didn't do it out of love.
   a. Judas   b. Judas Iscariot   c. Thomas

7. Jesus gave him to Mary his mother before he died.
   a. Peter   b. James   c. John

8. He put his hand in Jesus' side after the Resurrection.
   a. Thomas   b. John   c. Peter

9. He had an early breakfast with Peter, Thomas, James, and John. Jesus cooked.
   a. Andrew   b. Philip   c. Nathanael

10. He baptized an Ethiopian he met on the road.
    a. Philip   b. Simon   c. Thomas

ANSWERS

1. Andrew. Matthew 4:18

2. James. Matthew 4:22

3. Peter. Matthew 4:15

4. Matthew. Matthew 9:9

5. Peter. Matthew 14:29

6. Judas Iscariot. Luke 22:47

7. John. John 19:20-27

8. Thomas. John 20:27

9. Nathanael. John 21:2

10. Philip. Acts 8:38

? Of the 12 spies who were sent to explore Canaan, which two gave invasion a thumbs up?

Joshua and Caleb. Numbers 14:6-9

ROYAL ROOSTS

WHAT COUNTRY DID THESE PEOPLE RULE?

1. Candace

2. Nebuchadnezzar

3. Cyrus

4. Shalmaneser

5. Pharaoh (pick one)

6. Nero

7. Ben-Hadad

8. Evil-Merodach

9. Sennacherib

10. Og

ANSWERS

1. Candace was queen of the Ethiopians. Acts 8:27

2. Nebuchadnezzar was king of Babylon. 2 Kings 24:1

3. Cyrus was king of Persia. 2 Chronicles 36:22

4. Shalmaneser was king of Assyria. 2 Kings 17:3

5. Pharaoh (all of them) was king of Egypt. Genesis 41:46

6. Nero was the emperor of Rome.

7. Ben-Hadad was king of Syria. 1 Kings 20:1

8. Evil-Merodach was another king of Babylon. 2 Kings 25:27

9. Sennacherib was king of Assyria. 2 Chronicles 32:1

10. Og was king of Bashan. Numbers 21:33

REPEAT AFTER ME

When King David was old he was always cold, so he had a girl named Abishag to keep him warm and wait on him. 1 Kings 1:1-4

Three o'clock in the afternoon was prayertime in Paul's day. Acts 3:1

Samaria was built on a hill that was bought for about 150 pounds of silver. 1 Kings 16:24

•••••••••••

When Asa, King of Judah, was old
he got diseased feet. 1 Kings 15:23

•••••••••••

Once when Paul was speaking a man named Eutychus who was sitting in a window fell asleep and plunged three stories to the ground. He died, but Paul brought him back to life. Acts 20:9-12

"It is more blessed to give than to receive..." is a quote from Jesus that He never actually said in the Bible. Acts 20:35

Manna means "what is it."

Israel (Jacob) told his sons to take pistachio nuts to the ruler (Joseph) in Egypt. Genesis 43:11

Take Seven

There were seven, or seven pairs, of every clean animal on the ark. Genesis 7:2-4

Jacob worked for Laban for seven years to marry Rachel, or so he thought. Genesis 29:18

Joshua and his army marched around Jericho seven times on the seventh day with seven priests blowing seven trumpets. Joshua 6:3-4

Samson had seven braids in his hair. Judges 16:13

Jesus fed "The Crowd" with seven loaves of bread. Matthew 15:34

Jesus drove seven demons from Mary Magdalene. Mark 16:9

Seven were chosen from the disciples to distribute food to widows. Acts 6:3

Joseph predicted seven years of abundance and seven years of famine in Egypt. Exodus 12:15

Passover lasted for seven days. Exodus 12:15

Naaman was healed of leprosy by dipping into the Jordan River seven times. 2 Kings 5:14

Of course there are more seven-things, but you get the point.

Paul Slept Here

1. At this house in Philippi.

2. On this street when he was blind.

3. Where he left his coat with Carpus.

4. Where he sang with Silas.

5. Where he was stoned and left for dead.

6. In Thessalonica where a nasty mob tried to hunt him down.

7. Where the disciples lowered him in a basket so he could get out of town.

8. On Malta where his ship ran aground.

9. Where he and Barnabas "shook the dust from their feet."

10. Where he made tents with Aquila and Priscilla.

WHERE PAUL SLEPT

1. Lydia's house. Acts 16:14-15

2. Straight Street. Acts 9:11

3. Troas. 2 Timothy 4:13

4. Jail in Philippi. Acts 16:25

5. Lystra. Acts 14:19

6. Jason's house. Acts 17:5

7. Damascus. Acts 9:25

8. Publius' house. Acts 28:7

9. Pisidian Antioch. Acts 13:13-51

10. Corinth. Acts 18:1-3

? The Book of Philemon is a post card from Paul to Philemon. On whose behalf was it written?

Onesimus, Philemon's runaway servant.

WHO SAID THIS?

1. "Look, Lord! Here and now I give half of my possessions to the poor. . . ."

2. "I have never eaten anything impure or unclean."

3. "I have sinned against the Lord."

4. "I baptize you with water for repentance."

5. "Now, O Lord, take away my life, for it is better for me to die than to live."

6. "But as for me and my household, we will serve the Lord."

7. "I appeal to Caesar."

8. "I have sinned for I have betrayed innocent blood."

9. "Your father and I have been anxiously searching for you."

10. "Come, see a man who told me everything I ever did."

WE SAID IT

1. Zacchaeus. Luke 19:8

2. Peter. Acts 10:14

3. David. 2 Samuel 12:13

4. John the Baptist. Matthew 3:11

5. Jonah. Jonah 4:3

6. Joshua. Joshua 24:15

7. Paul. Acts 25:11

8. Judas Iscariot. Matthew 27:4

9. Mary. Luke 2:48

10. The Samaritan woman. John 4:29

? What is the last word in the Bible?
Amen. Revelation 22:21

Who's Crying Now

Esau cried when Jacob got their father's blessing.
Genesis 27:38

Joseph cried when he saw Benjamin in Egypt.
Genesis 43:30

Benjamin cried when he saw Joseph in Egypt.
Genesis 45:14

Joseph cried when he saw Jacob in Egypt. Genesis 46:29

Jacob cried when he saw. . .Well, let's not get carried away.

Samson's wife cried to get the answer to his riddle.
Judges 14:16

King Joash cried at Elisha's death bed. 2 Kings 13:14

Esther cried while convincing King Xerxes to get rid of Haman. Esther 8:3

Baby Moses cried when Pharaoh's daughter found him.
Exodus 2:6

In the gross category. . .Isaiah said the sword of the Lord was covered with fat from rams' kidneys and blood from lambs and goats. Isaiah 34:6

Aaron and Hur were the two guys who held up Moses' hands while Joshua's army fought the Amalekites. As long as his hands were in the air, the Israelites were winning. Exodus 17:12

Jephthah and the Gileadites guarded a spot of land by asking Ephraimites to say "Shibboleth." They were killed if they couldn't say it correctly. Judges 12:5-6

? Who is the "father of lies?"
The Devil. John 8:44

When the Israelites won the battle with the Midianites, they got 675,000 sheep, 61,000 donkeys, and 32,000 "clean" women. Numbers 31:32-35

Jonathan once killed a huge man who had six fingers on each hand and six toes on each foot. 2 Samuel 21:20-21

Miriam, Moses' sister, had leprosy for seven days. Numbers 12:10

THE TEN COMMANDMENTS

Very simply, list the Ten Commandments. There's a Mercedes in it for you if you get them in order.

1. _____.

2. _____.

3. _____.

4. _____.

5. _____.

6. _____.

7. _____.

8. _____.

9. _____.

10. _____.

THE TEN COMMANDMENTS
IN ORDER
EXODUS 20:3-17

Just kidding about the Mercedes. Don't be so greedy.

1. You shall have no other gods before me.

2. You shall not make for yourself an idol.

3. You shall not misuse the name of the Lord your God.

4. Remember the Sabbath day by keeping it holy.

5. Honor your father and your mother.

6. You shall not murder.

7. You shall not commit adultery.

8. You shall not steal.

9. You shall not give false testimony against your neighbor.

10. You shall not covet anything belonging to your neighbor.

MORE TEN COMMANDMENT STUFF
2 PARTS OF PART 2

A: Which of the Ten Commandments are not mentioned in the New Testament, either by Jesus, Paul, or the Gospel writers?

1. _____.

2. _____.

3. _____.

4. _____.

Hint: There appear to be four.

B: What is the greatest commandment in the Law?
(This is not trivial, but it should make you think a bit.)

_____

_____

_____

Answers To 2 Parts of Part 2

A

1. You shall have no other gods before me. Exodus 20:3

2. You shall not make for yourself an idol. 20:4

3. You shall not misuse the name of the Lord your God. 20:7

4. Remember the Sabbath day by keeping it holy. 20:8

B

Matthew 22:37: Love the Lord your God
with all your heart and with all your soul
and with all your mind.

Casting Lots

During various times in the Bible, people cast lots to help them make decisions. They believed, in many cases, that the outcome was actually determined by God, so this is hardly a case for Atlantic City. A few examples:

The scapegoat was chosen that way. Leviticus 16:8

Joshua cast lots to distribute land to all the Israelite tribes. Joshua 18:10

Sailors cast lots to find out who was responsible for a big storm. It turned out to be Jonah. Jonah 1:7

The disciples cast lots to choose a replacement for Judas. Acts 1:26

The Israelites cast lots to figure out when each family was supposed to bring wood to burn at the altar. Nehemiah 10:34

Soldiers cast lots for Jesus' clothes. Matthew 27:35

David cast lots to choose heads of certain families who would minister. 1 Chronicles 24:5

Musicians cast lots to decide their responsibilities. 1 Chronicles 25:8

Lots were cast by families to choose gate keepers in Jerusalem. No wonder. Who would volunteer for the Dung gate, anyway? 1 Chronicles 26:3

GRACE NOTES

During the whole time the Israelites wandered around the desert, they never got swollen feet. Deuteronomy 8:4

The Ammonites were a stench in David's nostrils. 2 Samuel 10:6

Paul once healed a man who had dysentery. How nice of him. Acts 28:8

The next time you see a picture of Noah's family looking young and agile, look twice. Shem was 98 when the flood came. Genesis 11:10

Adam and Eve made the first clothes out of fig leaves. Genesis 3:8

There are 12 books of the Bible that start with J.

Moses hit a rock and got water when he was just supposed to talk to it. That's why he wasn't allowed to move to Canaan. Numbers 20:13

Saul had a seance once led by a medium from Endor. They called up Samuel from the dead. Don't try this at home. 1 Samuel 28:11

WHODUNIT?

WHO RAISED THESE PEOPLE FROM THE DEAD?

1. The son of the widow at Zarephath.
   a. Elijah   b. Elisha   c. Jeremiah

2. The son of the Shunammite woman who sneezed seven times when he was brought back to life.
   a. Elijah   b. Elisha   c. Jeremiah

3. The only son of the widow of Nain.
   a. Paul   b. Peter   c. Jesus

4. The 12-year-old daughter of Jairus, a ruler of the synagogue.
   a. Peter   b. Jesus   c. Paul

5. Lazarus, who was called from the tomb after four days.
   a. Peter   b. Jesus   c. Paul

6. Tabitha (Dorcas) from Joppa.
   a. Peter   b. Jesus   c. Paul

7. Eutychus, the guy who went to sleep and fell out of a three-story window.
   a. Peter   b. Jesus   c. Paul

THEY DID!

1. Elijah. 1 Kings 17:17-23

2. Elisha. 2 Kings 4:32-35

3. Jesus. Luke 7:11-17

4. Jesus. Luke 8:40-56

5. Jesus. John 11:1-44

6. Peter. Acts 9:36-43

7. Paul. Acts 20:9-12

? Who were Jesus' brothers by birth, or half-birth?
James, Joseph, Jr., Simon, and Judas. Matthew 13:15

VERILY I SAY TO YOU

To whom was Jesus speaking when he said. . .

1. Come down immediately. I must stay at your house today.

2. Woman, why are you crying?

3. Didn't you know I had to be in my Father's house?

4. Before the rooster crows today, you will disown me three times.

5. Mary has chosen what is better, and it will not be taken away from her.

6. For God so loved the world that he gave his one and only Son, that whoever believes in him shall not perish but have eternal life.

7. Here is a true Israelite, in whom there is nothing false.

8. Come, follow me, and I will make you fishers of men.

9. Are you still so dull?

10. You would have no power over me if it were not given to you from above.

ANSWERS

1. Zaccheus. Luke 9:5

2. Mary Magdalene. John 20:15

3. Joseph and Mary. Luke 2:49

4. Peter. Luke 22:61

5. Martha. Luke 10:42

6. Nicodemus. John 3:16

7. Nathanael. John 1:47

8. Peter and Andrew. Matthew 4:19

9. The disciples. Matthew 16:13

10. Pontius Pilate. John 19:11

? To whom was 3 John addressed?
Somebody named Gaius, John's friend. 3 John 1

MEDIUM RARE

Have you seen the writing on the wall? King Belshazzar did. When he was drinking out of a goblet from Jerusalem's temple, a hand wrote a message on his wall.
Daniel 5:5

Moses smashed the tablets of the Ten Commandments, so God had to make another set. Exodus 34:1

The Israelites wore tassels on their clothes to remind them of God's commandments. Numbers 15:38

The city of Ephesus was the guardian of the temple of Artemis, a fertility god. Acts 19:35

• • • • • • • • • • •

David pretended to be insane once by marking up a door and drooling all over his face.
1 Samuel 21:13

• • • • • • • • • • •

When the Israelites first checked out Canaan, they found grapevines so full it took two men to carry a single cluster.
Numbers 13:23

A beautiful, indiscreet woman is like a gold ring in a pig's snout. Proverbs 11:22

Jacob made the coat that he gave to Joseph, his favorite son.
Genesis 37:3

Down For The Count
(OF 12!)

Ishmael had 12 sons who were tribal rulers. Genesis 17:20

Jacob had 12 sons, too. You know who they were.
Genesis 49:28

The Sea in Solomon's temple stood on 12 bulls. 1 Kings 7:25

Elisha plowed with 12 yoke of oxen. 1 Kings 19:19

Jesus called 12 disciples. Matthew 10:1

There were 12 baskets full of leftovers when Jesus fed a crowd of people. Matthew 14:20

The New Jerusalem will have 12 gates guarded by twelve angels. Revelation 21:12

Moses sent 12 spies into Canaan. Numbers 13:1-15

A Levite cut his dead concubine up into 12 pieces, one for each tribe of Israel. That wasn't very nice. Judges 19:29

JUDGMENT DAY

Complete the acrostic with the names of the major judges. O.K., so it's misspelled. God must not have known any qualified people with U names.

1. J _ _ _ _ _ _ _

2. O _ _ _ _ _ _

3. D _ _ _ _ _ _ _

4. G _ _ _ _ _

5. E _ _ _

6. S _ _ _ _ _

ANSWERS

1. Jephthah, the one who sacrificed his daughter.

2. Othniel, Caleb's little brother who got Israel away from Mesopotamia.

3. Deborah, the woman who accompanied Barak into battle.

4. Gideon, the one who distributed Bibles. Just kidding.

5. Ehud, who killed fat King Eglon with a home made sword.

6. Samson, the strong one with long hair.

STAND BY YOUR MAN

Match the women to the men they were either married to or associated with.

1. Abigail   A. Abraham

2. Abital   B. David

3. Ahinoam   C. Jacob

4. Bathsheba

5. Bilhah

6. Eglah

7. Hagar

8. Haggith

9. Keturah

10. Leah

11. Maacah

12. Michal

13. Rachel

14. Sarah

15. Zilpah

ANSWERS

1. Abigail and David

2. Abital and David

3. Ahinoam and David

4. Bathsheba and David

5. Bilhah and Jacob

6. Eglah and David

7. Hagar and Abraham

8. Haggith and David

9. Keturah and Abraham

10. Leah and Jacob

11. Maacah and David

12. Michal and David

13. Rachel and Jacob

14. Sarah and Abraham

15. Zilpah and Jacob

Have A Clue

Myrrh is a gum resin.

Frankincense is a combination of gum and spices.

Flux is the same as violent dysentery. Acts 28:8

A testament, as in Old and New, is a statement of belief and/or evidence that something happened.

An ebenezer is a memorial stone. 1 Samuel 4:1

The next time you wear a shawl, you will be wearing a wimple. Ruth 3:15

Papyrus is writing paper made from a papyrus plant.

Cherubim are winged creatures that are half man and half animal.

Seraphim is the plural of the angel-types that Isaiah talked about.

PILLARS OF SALT
(OR A LOT ABOUT NOTHING)

Gamaliel was a famous teacher in Jerusalem who taught Paul everything he knew about a few things. Acts 22:3

Obadiah hid 100 prophets in caves and gave them food and water. 1 Kings 18:4

When Sennacherib and his army were camped outside Jerusalem one night, the angel of the Lord quietly killed 185,000 of them. Have a nice evening. 2 Kings 19:35

Abraham wasn't circumcised until he was 99 years old. Genesis 17:24

The next time you say, "Eat, drink and be merry," remember it was a fool who said it first. Luke 12:19

If Samson loved his wife enough to kill for her, why did he call her a cow? Read Judges 14:18

When the Benjamites were short on women, they went to a festival where each man caught one to take home. Judges 21:23

Isaac means "he laughed."

Say It Again, Sam

Who said. . .

1. Why have you disturbed me by bringing me up?

2. How can a man be born when he is old?

3. I am innocent of this man's blood.

4. No. You shall never wash my feet.

5. Jesus, remember me when you come into your kingdom.

6. He must become greater; I must become less.

7. Rabbi, I want to see.

8. I'll draw water for your camels, too, until they have finished drinking.

9. Samson, the Philistines are upon you!

10. You will not surely die.

Answers

1. Samuel, when Saul called him up from the grave. 1 Samuel 28:15

2. Nicodemus to Jesus. John 3:4

3. Pontius Pilate. Matthew 27:24

4. Peter. John 13:8

5. The thief on the cross. Luke 23:42

6. John the Baptist. John 3:30

7. Bartimaeus. Mark 10:51

8. Rebekah. Genesis 24:44

9. Delilah. Judges 16:9

10. The serpent. Genesis 3:4

• • • • • • • • • • • •

*God made the shadow on a sundial go back
ten steps as a sign to Hezekiah. 2 Kings 20:11*

THE GOOD, THE BAD, AND THE ABYSMAL

A few kings are listed below. Your job, should you decide to accept it: Which ones did right and which did evil in the eyes of the Lord? Then choose which kingdom they ruled, Israel or Judah.

1. Rehoboam

2. Asa

3. Nadab

4. Jehoshaphat

5. Omri

6. Ahaziah

7. Jehoahaz

8. Ahaz

9. Amaziah

10. Manasseh

ANSWERS

1. Rehoboam was evil in Judah.

2. Asa was good in Judah.

3. Nadab was evil in Israel.

4. Jehoshaphat was good in Judah.

5. Omri was evil in Israel.

6. Ahaziah was evil in Israel.

7. Jehoahaz was evil in Israel.

8. Ahaz was good in Judah.

9. Amaziah was good in Judah.

10. Manasseh was evil in Judah.

SOME MORE THREES

The wisemen gave baby Jesus three things—gold, frankincense, and myrrh. Matthew 2:11

The Holy Place in the Tabernacle had three things–the lampstand, the wood table, and the consecrated bread. Hebrews 9:2

Noah's three sons were Shem, Ham, and Japheth. Genesis 7:13

Job had three "comforting" friends. Job 4:1; 8:1; 11:1

Daniel had three friends—Shadrach, Meshach, and Abednego. Daniel 1:6

Noah's ark had three stories. Genesis 6:16

Esau had three wives—Judith, Basemath, and Mahalath. Genesis 26:34; 28:9

Jochebed's three children were Aaron, Miriam, and Moses. Various places in Exodus.

MORE PILLARS OF SALT

Esau was sometimes called Edom, which means red.
Genesis 25:30

In a battle, fighting men from Judah caught a man named Adoni-Bezek and cut off his fingers and big toes. Judges 1:6

There are 590 words in Obadiah. You can count them if you want to.

When Nebuchadnezzar went insane, he grew claws like a bird, feathers like an eagle, and ate grass like a cow. Daniel 4:33

While Ishmael lived in the desert with his mom, he learned to be an archer. Genesis 21:20

Samson killed more people when he died than he did when he lived. Judges 16:30

Abraham had slaves. Genesis 17:27

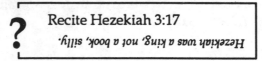

? Recite Hezekiah 3:17

Hezekiah was a king, not a book, silly.

THE 12 TRIBES OF ISRAEL

Place the names of the tribes of Israel in their designated land allotments. There are, as you know, only 12 tribes and 14 sections of land, so think hard.

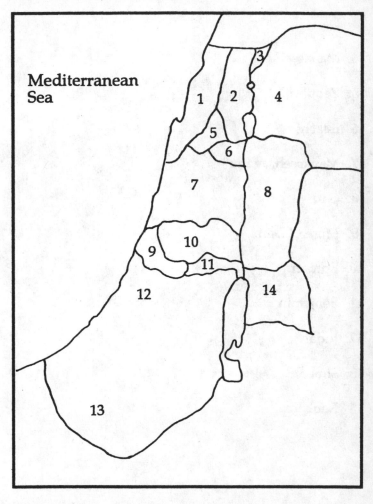

MAP ANSWERS

1. Asher

2. Naphtali

3. Dan

4. Manasseh

5. Zebulun

6. Issachar

7. Manasseh, again.

8. Gad

9. More of Dan

10. Ephraim

11. Benjamin

12. Judah

13. Simeon

14. Reuben

MATCH THE 'ITES

1. Gilonite

2. Tishbite

3. Canaanite

4. Hittite

5. Jebusite

6. Ammonite

7. Moabite

8. Amorite

9. Levite

10. Gileadite

A. Uriah

B. Araunah

C. Mamre

D. Aaron

E. Elijah

F. Ahithopel

G. Shua

H. Jephthah

I. Nahash

J. Ruth

MATCHED 'ITES

1. F. Ahithopel, David's counselor who sided with Absalom. 2 Samuel 15:12

2. E. Elijah, the prophet who was taken to heave. 1 Kings 17:1

3. G. Shua, Judah's father-in-law. Genesis 38:2

4. A. Uriah, Bathsheba's departed husband. 2 Samuel 11:6

5. B. Araunah. David saw the Angel of the Lord on his threshing floor. 1 Chronicles 21:15

6. I. Nahash, who wanted to remove the right eye of everyone in Jabesh Gilead. 1 Samuel 11:1

7. J. Ruth. Ruth 1:4

8. C. Mamre, an associate of Abraham. Genesis 14:13

9. D. Aaron, Moses' brother. Exodus 4:14

10. H. Jephthah, the judge who fought the Ammonites. Judges 11:1

Look Unto the Hills

When the Israelites were about to possess Canaan, they were to give blessings from Mount Gerizim and curses from Mount Ebal. Deuteronomy 11:29

Aaron died on Mount Hor. Numbers 20:29

Moses saw all of the Promised Land from Mount Nebo. Deuteronomy 34:1

Elijah proved the power of God in a contest with Baal worshipers on Mount Carmel. 1 Kings 18:19

Solomon built the temple on Mount Moriah. 2 Chronicles 3:1

Jesus gave the Beatitudes from a mountainside. You know–the Sermon on the Mount. Matthew 5:1

Abraham almost sacrificed Isaac on a mountain in Moriah. Genesis 22:2

God gave Moses the Ten Commandments on Mount Sinai. Exodus 19:3

ETC.

King Jehoiakim was really Eliakim. An Egyptian Pharoah changed his name. 2 Kings 23:34

Jesus called James and John "Sons of Thunder." Mark 3:17

As a curse, Joshua made the Gibeonites serve as woodcutters and water carriers for the Israelites. Joshua 9:23

• • • • • • • • • • •

It takes 11 days to go from Horeb to Kadesh Barnea by the Mount Seir road. They must not have had a jeep. Deuteronomy 1:2

• • • • • • • • • • •

The new earth won't have oceans. Revelation 21:1

Moses had two sons, Gershom and Eliezer. Exodus 18:3

Gehazi, a servant, lied to Elisha and got leprosy. 2 Kings 5:27

God killed Er, Tamar's first husband, because he was wicked. Genesis 38:7

Daniel was renamed Belteshazzar by the Babylonians. Daniel 1:7

ARE YOU MY MOTHER?

Their fathers are famous Bible characters, but do you know their mothers? Fill in the blanks.

1. Solomon, David and _____ son.

2. Samuel, Elkanah and _____ son.

3. Joseph, Jacob and _____ son.

4. Judah, Jacob and _____ son.

5. Obed, Boaz and _____ son.

6. Adonijah, David and _____ son.

7. Ahaziah, Ahab and _____ son.

8. Ishmael, Abraham and _____ son.

9. Jonathan, Saul and _____ son.

10. Eliphaz, Esau and _____ son.

ANSWERS

1. Bathsheba. 2 Samuel 12:24

2. Hannah. 1 Samuel 1:20

3. Rachel. Genesis 30:22-24

4. Leah. Genesis 29:35

5. Ruth. Ruth 4:17

6. Haggith. 1 Kings 1:5

7. Athaliah. 2 Kings 8:26

8. Hagar. Genesis 16:15

9. Ahinoam. 1 Samuel 14:49-50

10. Adah. Genesis 36:4

? Which "Marys" were at the cross?
Mary, Jesus' mother; Mary Magdalene; Mary,
James' mother; and Mary, Clopas' wife.
John 19:25; Mark 15:40

SIBLING RIVALRY?

Some are brothers, some are sisters, some are half of each.

1. Jesus called them when they were fishing.

2. One was a farmer and one was a shepherd.

3. One brother had the other one killed for violating their sister.

4. Jacob might have called these sisters the beauty and the beast.

5. These twins exchanged a birthright for a bowl of stew.

6. Jesus called these sons of Zebedee, too.

7. They were half-brothers whose descendants fought on a regular basis.

8. This married couple tended to laugh at the wrong times.

9. These brothers of Ham covered up their dad under exposing circumstances.

10. These sisters of Lazarus were very attentive to Jesus.

ANSWERS

1. Simon Peter and Andrew. Matthew 4:18

2. Cain and Abel. Genesis 4:1-2

3. Absalom and Ammon. 2 Samuel 13

4. Rachel and Leah. Genesis 29:16

5. Jacob and Esau. Genesis 25:22-36

6. James and John. Matthew 4:21

7. Isaac and Ishmael. Genesis 16:15; 21:3

8. Abraham and Sarah. Genesis 20:12

9. Shem and Japheth. Genesis 9:23

10. Mary and Martha. John 12:1-3

 Saul had a son named Jonathan, of course. But can you name his four other children?

Ishvi, Malki-Shua, Merab, and Michal. 1 Samuel 17:4

DO YOU WANT TO KNOW
A SECRET?

Goliath was over nine feet tall. 1 Samuel 17:4

Before a girl could be presented to King Xerxes, she had to put up with 12 months of beauty treatments. Esther 2:12

The Philistines offered gold rats as a guilt offering. Thanks a lot! 1 Samuel 6:18

Boaz gave Ruth and Naomi a load of barley as a present. Ruth 3:15

Samuel's mother made him a little robe every year while he was living with Eli. 1 Samuel 2:19

Jesus was trying to be alone to mourn the death of John the Baptist when the crowd of 5000-plus found him. Surprise! Matthew 14:13

Moses was more humble than anybody. Numbers 12:3

David's bodyguard Benaiah killed a lion in the snow. 1 Chronicles 11:23

TENFOLD

God gave Ten Commandments. Exodus 20:3-17

David took ten loaves of bread and ten cheeses to his brothers who were fighting the Philistines. 1 Samuel 17:17

There were ten basins, ten gold candlesticks, and ten tables in the temple. 2 Chronicles 4:6-8

Haman, from the book of Esther, had ten sons. Esther 9:14

A ten-acre vineyard will produce only a bath of wine, or about six gallons. Isaiah 5:10

Jesus told a story about ten virgins who were waiting for the bridegroom. Matthew 25:1

Then He told about a woman who had ten silver coins and lost one. Luke 15:8

Then He told another one about a man who gave ten minas to ten servants. Luke 19:13

Jesus healed ten lepers. Luke 17:12

THE 2000 LITTLE PIGS
(AND OTHER TRUE STORIES!)

Once Jesus called demons out of a man and sent them into a herd of about 2000 pigs. Mark 5:13

When the kings of Sodom and Gomorrah ran away from their enemies, they got stuck in some tar pits. Genesis 14:10

After Haman was hanged on the gallows, King Xerxes hanged his sons, too. Esther 9:14

• • • • • • • • • • •

Aaron's hunchbacked descendants couldn't offer food to God. Leviticus 21:20

• • • • • • • • • • •

Solomon's throne had six steps and a gold footstool attached to it. 2 Chronicles 9:18

Some city officials put Jeremiah in a mud hole to starve to death. Jeremiah 38:6

There are seven different Jeremiahs in the Bible. 1 Chronicles 5:24; 12:4, 10, 13; 2 Kings 23:30; Jeremiah 1:1; 35:3

When God needed to punish David, he gave him three choices: three years of famine, three months of enemy pursuit, or three days of plague. Which would you choose? 2 Samuel 24:13

Jephtnah's mother was a prostitute. Judges 11:1

David's son Absalom conspired to get the throne from his father. 2 Samuel 15

Gideon had 71 sons. Judges 8:30

? Elijah didn't die, as you know. Who else was "taken away?"

Enoch, Methuselah's dad. Genesis 5:24

Samson killed a thousand men with a donkey's jawbone. Judges 15:16

Paul circumcised Timothy. Acts 16:3

Abraham sent 318 men to rescue Lot from captivity. Genesis 14:14-16

God struck Uzzah dead when he touched the ark of the covenant. The poor guy was trying to keep the ark from falling off its cart. 2 Samuel 6:7

Shamgar, one of the judges, killed 600 Philistines with an oxgoad. Judges 3:31

It's a Trivial Thing

Judah had as many gods as they did towns.
Jeremiah 11:13

When the Lord opened the seventh seal in John's vision, all of heaven was quiet for about half an hour.
Revelation 8:1

God smelled Noah's burnt offering after the flood.
Genesis 8:21

Isaiah said, "The Lord will whistle for flies from Egypt and bees from Assyria." Picture it. Isaiah 7:18

Solomon's girlfriend had to take care of the vineyards because her brothers were mad at her. Solomon 1:6

Some descendants of priests couldn't find their family records, so they weren't allowed to be priests. Unclean!
Ezra 1:62

Abraham's father Terah died in Haran. Haran was the name of Terah's son who died in Ur. Genesis 11:28, 32

Esther was given seven maids even before she was made the queen. Esther 2:9

When Nehemiah found out that some Hebrew men had married foreign women, he beat them and pulled out their hair. Nehemiah 13:25

John wrote the book of Revelation to seven churches in Asia. Revelation 1:4

When Jesus drove out a mute demon from a mute man, the man was able to speak. Luke 11:14

The Lord used the king of Assyria as a razor to shave the legs of the people of Judah. Isaiah 7:20

King Nebuchadnezzar made Daniel chief of magicians, enchanters, astrologers, and diviners. Daniel 5:11

A man named Simon tried to pay Peter and John for the power to give people the Holy Spirit. Acts 8:19

Zechariah saw a vision of a woman trapped in a basket that was carried away by two women with wings.
Zechariah 5:6-9

The Lord showed Amos a bowl full of ripe fruit—ripe like Israel was for judgment. Amos 8:1-2

WAS IT "PSALM"-THING I SAID?

David had a way with words. Fill in the missing ones in this quiz from the Psalms.

1. Their throat is an _____ _____, with their tongue they speak deceit.

2. Oh Lord, our Lord, how majestic is _____ _____.

3. . . .My God is my rock in whom _____ _____ _____.

4. Remember not the sins of _____ _____.

5. The voice of the Lord is _____; the voice of the Lord is _____.

6. _____and see that the Lord is good.

7. Sing to the Lord a _____ _____, for he has done marvelous _____.

8. They repay me evil for _____, and hatred for my _____.

9. I lift up my eyes to the _____—where does my _____ come from?

10. Your word, O Lord, is _____; it stands firm in the _____.

ANSWERS

1. open grave. 5:9

2. your name. 8:1

3. I take refuge. 18:2

4. my youth. 25:6

5. powerful, majestic. 29:4

6. taste. 34:8

7. new song, things. 98:19

8. good, friendship. 109:5

9. hills, help. 121:1

10. eternal, heavens. 119:89

? Who killed Jonathan, Saul's son?

The Philistines. 1 Chronicles 10:2

Who Said?

1. "Give me wisdom and knowledge, that I may lead this people. . ."

2. "Am I a dog that you come at me with sticks?"

3. "Whom are you pursuing? A dead dog? A flea?"

4. "When will you end these speeches? Be sensible, and then we can talk."

5. "You are a child of the devil; and an enemy of every thing that is right."

6. "Don't be afraid, for I will surely show you kindness for the sake of your father Jonathan."

7. "O Lord, my God, have you brought tragedy also upon this widow I am staying with by causing her son to die?"

8. "My father! My father! The chariots and horsemen of Israel."

9. "Worthy is the Lamb who was slain, to receive power and wealth and wisdom and strength and honor and glory and praise."

10. "Naked I came from my mother's womb, and naked I will depart."

ANSWERS

1. Solomon. 2 Chronicles 1:10

2. Goliath. 1 Samuel 17:43

3. David to Saul. 1 Samuel 24:14

4. Bildad to Job. Job 18:2

5. Paul. Acts 13:10

6. David to Mephibosheth. 2 Samuel 9:7

7. Elijah. 1 Kings 17:20

8. Elisha. 2 Kings 2:116

9. More angels than John could count. Revelation 5:12

10. Job. Job 1:21

SACKCLOTH IS IN

King Hezekiah tore his clothes and put on sackcloth and went into the temple. Isaiah 37:1

The king of Nineveh put it on and sat in the dust. He even covered his animals with it. Jonah 3:6-7

David said, "I put on sackcloth and humbled myself with fasting." Psalm 35:13

Mordecai put it on when he found out that Haman ordered all the Jews to be killed. Esther 4:1

Jacob put on sackcloth when he thought Joseph had been eaten by an animal. Genesis 37:34

Job wore sackcloth during his time of torment. Job 16:15

In Jeremiah's day, people put scarecrows in melon patches. Jeremiah 10:5

A rainbow surrounded a throne in heaven while John was watching "in the spirit." Revelation 4:13

Ham was the father of Canaan. Genesis 9:18

John ate a scroll that was as sweet as honey but made his stomach sour. Well, of course. Revelation 10:10

? Who said, "I know where you live"?

Revelation 2:13
Jesus, about the church in Pergamum.

The two days of Purim are celebrated to recall the Hebrew's victorious two-day battle against enemies while Esther was queen. Esther 9:18-28

Every morning Job sacrificed a burnt offering just in case one of his children had sinned. What a dad! Job 1:5

David had 20 children. 1 Chronicles 3:1-9

AND GOD SAID. . .

"let there be light" and many other things. List the results of God's creation in order of their occurrence.

1.

2.

3.

4.

5.

6.

7.

ANSWERS

Genesis 1:1-1:2

1. On the first day, God created light.

2. On the second day, God separated land from water.

3. On the third day, God created vegetation.

4. On the fourth day, God created the sun, moon, and stars.

5. On the fifth day, God created marine life and birds.

6. On the sixth day, God created land animals and people.

7. On the seventh day, God created rest.

AND THEN GOD SAID

To whom was God speaking when He said. . .

1. "As long as the earth endures, seedtime and harvest, cold and heat, summer and winter, day and night will never cease."

2. "Son of man, tremble as you eat your food, and shudder in fear as you drink your water."

3. "Can you pull in the leviathan with a fishhook or tie down his tongue with a rope?"

4. "With the three hundred men that lapped I will save you and give the Midianites into your hands."

5. "See, I am about to do something in Israel that will make the ears of everyone who hears of it tingle."

6. "Take again the equipment of a foolish shepherd."

7. "Get up and go into Damascus. There you will be told all that you have been assigned to do."

8. "I will have mercy on whom I will have mercy, and I will have compassion on whom I will have compassion."

9. "You will shepherd my people Israel, and you will become their ruler."

10. "I have seen this people, and they are a stiff-necked people indeed."

ANSWERS

1. Noah. Genesis 8:22

2. Ezekiel. Ezekiel 12:18

3. Job. Job 41:2

4. Gideon. Judges 7:7

5. Samuel. 1 Samuel 3:11

6. Zechariah. Zechariah 11:15

7. Paul. Acts 22:10

8. Moses. Exodus 33:19

9. David. 2 Samuel 5:2

10. Moses. Deuteronomy 9:13

When Fools Rush In

Wise sayings about the foolish.

A fool will be a servant to the wise. Proverbs 11:29

A fool exposes his folly. Proverbs 4:16

It's better to meet a bear robbed of her cubs than one.
Proverbs 17:12

To have one for a son brings grief. Proverbs 17:21

When one speaks a proverb, it's like a lame man's legs that
just hang there. Proverbs 26:7

A fool shows everyone how stupid he is.
Ecclesiastes 10:3

A fool delights in airing his own opinions. Proverbs 18:2

A fool repeats his foolishness like a dog returns to his
vomit. Proverbs 26:11

MISH MASH

When Jeremiah wrote scrolls to be read to Jehoiakim, he dictated them to Baruch, his secretary. Jeremiah 36:4

John heard a voice like a trumpet while on the island of Patmos. Revelation 1:10

God inflicted Pharaoh with diseases for taking Abram's wife. Genesis 12:17

Amos prophesied two years before an earthquake.
Amos 1:1

The new Jerusalem will never get dark. Revelation 21:25

When Jewish exiles left Persia to build the temple in Jerusalem, they took 30 gold dishes, 1,000 silver dishes, 29 silver pans, 30 gold bowls, and 410 silver bowls.
Bon voyage. Ezra 1:9-10

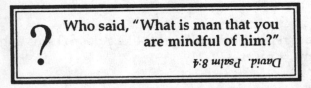

? Who said, "What is man that you are mindful of him?"

David. Psalm 8:4

Jashobeam, Eleazar, and Shammah were known as "the three." They were David's mightiest men.
1 Chronicles 11:11-12, 2 Samuel 23:11

A IS FOR APPLE—

or is it? Find just a few of the "A" names found in the Bible.

```
A A N D R E W O R A A
P B A H A H A Z B A D
A I A G U M Z I A R O
B S P Y S O M A T O N
I H L E M E B B H N I
G A U A L R O E A A J
A G D E A N H D L Q A
I A C H A P A N I U H
L H A H A R B E A I D
F M C S Z V E G H L A
G A A B S A L O M A T
```

Aaron	Amos	Andrew
Abednego	Abel	Aquila
Abigail	Athaliah	Abimelech
Asaph	Abraham	Adonijah
Absalom	Abishag	Achan
Ahab	Adam	Ahaz

WORDSEARCH SOLUTION

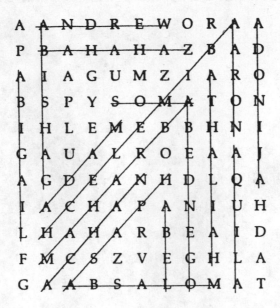

```
A A N D R E W O R A A
P B A H A H A Z B A D
A I A G U M Z I A R O
B S P Y S O M A T O N
I H L E M E B B H N I
G A U A L R O E A A J
A G D E A N H D L Q A
I A C H A P A N I U H
L H A H A R B E A I D
F M C S Z V E G H L A
G A A B S A L O M A T
```

I Feel A Song Comin' On

Who composed these songs found in the Scripture?

1. "Her hand reached for the tent peg, her right hand for the workman's hammer."

2. "From now on all generations will call me blessed. . ."

3. "And you, my child, will be called a prophet of the Most High."

4. "By the blast of your nostrils the waters piled up."

5. "Keep me safe, O God, for in you I take refuge."

6. "I will sing for the one I love, a song about his vineyard. . ."

7. "The Lord brings death and makes alive; he brings down to the grave and raises up."

8. "Glory to God in the highest and on earth peace to men on whom his favor rests."

9. "The Lord is my rock, my fortress and my deliverer."

10. "Like arrows in the hands of a warrior are sons born in one's youth."

Answers

1. Deborah and Barak. Judges 5:26

2. Mary. Luke 1:46

3. Zechariah. Luke 1:76

4. Moses and the Israelites. Exodus 15:8

5. David. Psalm 16:1

6. Isaiah. Isaiah 5:1

7. Hannah. 1 Samuel 2:6

8. Heavenly Hosts. Luke 2:15

9. David. 2 Samuel 22:2

10. Solomon. Psalm 127:4

Pass the Fig Leaves, Please

A list of naked people.

Noah was naked after he fell down drunk. Genesis 9:21

Adam and Eve. Genesis 2:25

Death is naked before God. Ok, it's a thing, not a person. Job 26:6

A young man who had been following Jesus ran away naked when his loin cloth fell off. Mark 14:51-52

Seven sons of Sceva were attacked by a demon-possessed man, and they ran away bleeding and naked. Acts 19:16

Isaiah was stripped and barefoot for three years. 1 Samuel 20:3

When the men of Sodom tried to capture Lot's special guests, they were all struck blind. Genesis 19:11

In the new earth and heaven there isn't a sea.
Revelation 21:1

If you wink maliciously, you'll cause grief.
Proverbs 10:10

On the Sabbath day in Jerusalem, Nehemiah shut all the doors to the city so merchants couldn't violate Sabbath rules. Nehemiah 13:19

A woman named Sheerah built Lower and Upper Beth Horon. 1 Chronicles 7:24

Because Jehoraim was an evil king, God afflicted him with a disease of the bowels. Take that! 2 Chronicles 21:18

Noah only had seven days to gather up all the animals into the ark. Genesis 7:3-4

Zechariah saw a flying scroll 30 feet long and 15 feet wide.
In-coming! Zechariah 5:2

The Lord whistles for those at the ends of the earth.
Isaiah 5:26

GUESS WHO I AM

In this multiple choice quiz, choose the judge who fits the description.

A.	Othniel	B.	Ehud	C.	Shamgar
D.	Deborah	E.	Gideon	F.	Tola
G.	Jair	H.	Jephthah	I.	Samson

1. He blew his trumpet and smashed his empty jar.
   E   C   I

2. This left-handed judge stabbed a king with a home-made sword.
   B   F   I

3. This one killed 600 Philistines with an ox goad.
   C   E   G

4. This judge was Caleb's nephew.
   A   B   E

5. This one said, "With a donkey's jawbone I have made donkeys of them."
   I   A   C

6. He had 30 sons on 30 donkeys and controlled 30 towns.
   G   F   H

7. This judge sacrificed his only child because of a vow he made to the Lord.
   H   C   B

8. When Barak was afraid to confront an enemy alone, this judge went with him.
   D   B   H

ANSWERS

1. E. Gideon. Judges 7:19

2. B. Ehud. Judges 3:21

3. C. Shamgar. Judges 4:8-9

4. A. Othniel. Judges 3:9

5. I. Samson. Judges 15:16

6. G. Jair. Judges 10:4

7. H. Jephthah. Judges 11:30-39

8. D. Deborah. Judges 4:8-9

What's In A Name?

Unscramble the common and not-so-common biblical names for God.

1. hhimsgot (2 words)

2. gdjue

3. ysniectanfoda (3 words)

4. hdorewt (2 words)

5. dgeentrnlao (2 words)

6. ndngeadhtngnebieni (4 words)

7. hhvoaje

8. jbtoniofacpor (3 words)

9. relpefhoasio (3 words)

10. fogtimjcbaohynoe (4 words)

ANSWERS

1. Most High. Genesis 14:18-20

2. Judge. Genesis 18:25

3. Ancient of Days. Daniel 7:9

4. The Word. John 1:1

5. Eternal God. Genesis 21:33

6. Beginning and the End. Revelation 1:8

7. Jehovah.

8. Portion of Jacob. Jeremiah 10:16

9. Hope of Israel. Jeremiah 14:8

10. Mighty One of Jacob. Genesis 49:24

Four!

*No, you're not golfing, you're reading a list of
four-things in the Bible.*

The garden of Eden had four rivers. Genesis 2:10

If an Israelite stole someone's sheep, he had to pay it back with four sheep. Exodus 22:1

The ark of the covenant has four gold rings. Exodus 25:12

The lampstand had four cups shaped like almond flowers. Exodus 25:34

The Most Holy Place had a curtain hung with gold hooks on four posts that stood on four silver bases. Exodus 26:32

Jephthah's daughter spent four months with her friends before she was sacrificed. Judges 19:2

Elijah poured four jars of water on his offering when competing with followers of Baal, three times even. 1 Kings 18:33

Bathsheba and David had four children. 1 Chronicles 3:5

Ezekiel saw four living creatures each with four faces and four wings. Ezekiel 1:5-6

Honey, a Mean Wife, and Other Things

If you eat too much honey, you'll throw up. Proverbs 25:16

When Zechariah, John the Baptist's father, was mute, people seemed to think he was deaf, too. Luke 1:62

When Cain was banished from Eden, God put a mark on him so no one would kill him. Genesis 4:15

The new Jerusalem will be 1,400 miles long and 1,400 miles wide. Revelation 21:16

It's better to live on the roof than to live inside with a mean wife. Proverbs 21:9

? Of the three kings who reigned during the rebuilding of the temple in Jerusalem, who was in power when it was finished—Cyrus, Darius, or Artaxerxes?

Darius. Ezra 6:15

When Reuben slept with Jacob's concubine Bilhah, he lost his birthright to Joseph. Genesis 35:22, 1 Chronicles 5:1

Solomon's throne had six steps with twelve lions sitting on them. 2 Chronicles 9:18

I HAVE A DREAM

Who had these dreams?

1. He saw a statue whose feet were smashed by a stone.

2. Four winds of heaven stirred up the sea in this man's dream.

3. A giant tree had enough fruit for everybody.

4. They were warned in a dream about Herod's evil scheme.

5. He was warned to take his family to Egypt.

6. He saw angels going up and down on a ladder.

7. His brothers were annoyed with his dreams, one of which involved the moon and stars.

8. This ruler dreamed about some hefty cows eating some scrawny ones.

9. He saw a vine produce grapes and squeezed their juice into a cup.

10. She had an unpleasant dream and blamed it on Jesus.

ANSWERS

1. Nebuchadnezzar. Daniel 2:31-34

2. Daniel. Daniel 7:2

3. Nebuchadnezzar again. Daniel 4:10-12

4. The magi. Matthew 2:12

5. Joseph. Matthew 2:13

6. Jacob. Genesis 28:12

7. Joseph. Genesis 37:9

8. Pharaoh. Genesis 41:1-4

9. Pharoah's cup bearer. Genesis 40:9-11

10. Pilate's wife. Matthew 27:19

SOMETHING OLD...

After reading the New Testament quote, name the Old Testament passage to which it refers or even duplicates.

1. "...for out of you will come a ruler who will be the shepherd of my people Israel." Matthew 2:6

2. "You will be with child and give birth to a son, and you are to give him the name Jesus." Luke 1:31

3. "When they had crucified him, they divided up his clothes by casting lots. " Matthew 27:35

4. "But when they came to Jesus and found that he was already dead, they did not break his legs." John 19:33

5. "Jesus found a young donkey and sat upon it, as it is written, '...see, your king is coming, seated on a donkey's colt.'" John 12:14-15

6. "'What are you willing to give me if I hand him over to you?' so they counted out 30 pieces of silver." Matthew 26:15

7. "And the scripture was fulfilled which says, 'He was counted with the lawless ones.'" Mark 15:28

8. "The blind receive sight, the lame walk, and the deaf hear." Matthew 11:5

9. "A voice of one calling in the desert, 'Prepare the way of the Lord, make straight paths for him.'" Matthew 3:3

10. "But I, when I am lifted up from the earth, will draw all men to myself." John 12:32

ANSWERS

1. Micah 5:2

2. Isaiah 7:14

3. Psalm 22:18

4. Psalm 34:20

5. Zechariah 9:9

6. Zechariah 11:12

7. Isaiah 53:12

8. Isaiah 35:5-6

9. Isaiah 40:3

10. Isaiah 33:10

? Where did Job live?

Uz. Job 1:1

WOE IS ME

*All these people tore their clothes as a sign of distress
for one reason or another.*

Joshua and Caleb tore their clothes while trying to convince the people that Canaan was really attainable. Number 14:6

Joshua tore his when the Lord allowed the Israelites to lose in battle. Joshua 7:6

Jephthah tore his clothes when he realized that he had to sacrifice his daughter. Judges 11:35

David and his men tore theirs when they mourned for Saul and David. 2 Samuel 1:11

Tamar tore her robe after Amnon raped her. 2 Samuel 13:19

Ahab tore his for fear of being eaten by dogs. 1 Kings 21:27

King Joziah tore his when he heard the Book of the Law being read. 2 Kings 22:11

Mordecai tore his clothes when Haman plotted to kill the Jews. Esther 4:1

Paul and Barnabas tore their clothes when people in Lystra thought they were gods. Acts 14:14

When Paul needed to escape from Damascus, his friends lowered him from the city wall in a basket. Acts 9:25

It's better to be with a mad bear than with a fool. Proverbs 17:12

Once, David's mightiest men risked their lives to get him some water from a well, but David wouldn't drink it because of all the trouble they went to. 1 Chronicles 11:17-19

> **?** If a cheerful heart is good medicine,
> what does a crushed spirit do?
>
> Dry up the bones. Proverbs 17:22

When King David conquered Ammonite towns, he forced the occupants to labor with saws, picks, and axes. 1 Chronicles 20:3

Once the people in the synagogue in Nazareth were so disgusted with Jesus that they tried to throw him off of a cliff. Luke 4:29

Golgotha means "The Place of The Skulls." Mark 15:22

Gideon was also known as Jerub-Baal. Judges 7:1

Only priests could carry the ark of the covenant. 1 Corinthians 15:2

WILL THE REAL MARY. . .

Which Mary fits the description?
   A. Mary Magdalene
   B. Mary, Jesus' Mother
   C. Mary, the wife of Clopas
   D. Mary, Martha's Sister

1. This Mary poured expensive perfume on Jesus' feet and wiped it off with her hair.

2. Seven demons were driven out of this Mary.

3. These Marys were the first people to whom Jesus appeared after his resurrection.

4. Jesus handed John the apostle over to this Mary as a son.

5. This Mary was scolded for not helping to make dinner.

6. When this Mary's brother died, Jesus came to the rescue and brought him back to life.

ANSWERS

1. D. Mary, Martha's sister. John 11:2

2. A. Mary Magdalene. Luke 8:2

3. A, C. Mary Magdalene and Mary, the wife of Clopas.
   Mark 16:9

4. B. Mary, Jesus' mother. John 19:25

5. D. Mary, Martha's sister. Luke 10:40

6. D. Mary, Martha's sister. John 11:43

TRAVELIN' MAN

Label this map
and name
what Jesus
did in each place.

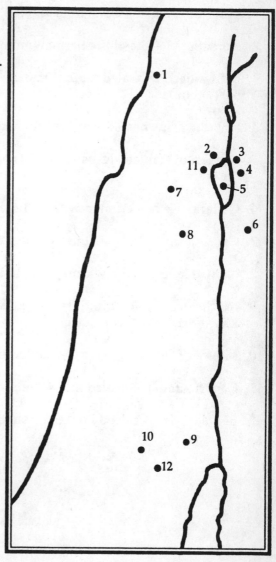

ANSWERS

1. Tyre. He healed a Canaanite woman's daugther.

2. Korazin. The site of the Sermon on the Mount.

3. Bethsaida. He healed a blind man and fed more than 5,000 people.

4. Khersa. Jesus healed a man with demons. Luke 8:26

5. The Sea of Galilee. Jesus walked on water and calmed the storm.

6. Gadara. He healed men with demons. Matthew 8:28

7. Cana. Jesus turned water into wine.

8. Nain. He restored a widow's son to life.

9. Jericho. He healed blind Bartimieus and called Zacchaeus down from a tree.

10. Mount of Olives. Jesus ascended into heaven.

11. Capernaum. He healed many people here.

12. Bethany. Jesus raised Lazarus from the dead.

Feed Me, Heal Me

If you stay awake, you'll have extra food. Proverbs 20:13

After David brought the ark back to Jerusalem, he gave a cake of raisins and cake of dates to each Israelite.
1 Chronicles 16:3

Once Jesus healed a mute man by spitting and touching the guy's tongue. Say ah. Mark 7:33

King Amaziah had 10,000 of his enemies killed by marching them off of a cliff. 2 Chronicles 25:12

?	When Jesus said, "Man does not live by bread alone, but on every word that comes from the mouth of God," what verse was he quoting?
	Deuteronomy 8:3 (Mark 4:4)

People were healed just by touching Jesus' clothes.
Mark 6:56

Hosanna means "save now."

DRESSED FOR SUCCESS

Jermiah wore a linen belt that couldn't get wet.
Jeremiah 13:1

In a vision, Joshua wore a clean turban to show that his sins
had been taken away. Zechariah 3:4-5

Israelite priests wore a breast piece, an ephod, a robe, a
tunic, a turban, and a sash. Exodus 28:4

Early Christian women wore head coverings when they
prayed and prophesied. 1 Corinthians 11:5

Early Christian men didn't. 1 Corinthians 11:4

Israelites wore tassels on their clothes to remind them of
God's commands. Numbers 15:37-41

OH, THOSE PROPHETS

They had so much to say. Which one said each of these gems?

1. "Dry bones, hear the word of the Lord."

2. "Beat your plowshares into swords and your pruning hooks into spears."

3. "Seaweed was wrapped around my head."

4. "The Lord is God, a refuge in times of trouble."

5. "They will beat their swords into plowshares and their spears into pruning hooks."

6. "For He (the Lord) will be like a refiner's fire or a launderer's soap."

7. "Holy, holy, holy is the Lord Almighty; the whole earth is full of his glory."

8. "The heart is deceitful above all things and beyond cure. Who can understand it."

9. "Give us nothing but vegetables to eat and water to drink."

10. "Hear this word, you cows of Bashan on Mount Samaria, you women who oppress the poor and crush the needy."

ANSWERS

1. Ezekiel. Ezekiel 37:4

2. Joel. Joel 3:10

3. Jonah. Jonah 2:5

4. Nahum. Nahum 1:7

5. Micah. Micah 4:3

6. Malachi. Malachi 3:2

7. Isaiah. Isaiah 6:3

8. Jeremiah. Jeremiah 17:9

9. Daniel. Daniel 1:12

10. Amos. Amos 4:1

CRAZY CROSSWORD

Fill in the squares with two verses from the New Testament. No, not just any verses. Here are some clues. 1. All the Ws have been given. 2. These verses are an introduction of sorts written by someone whom Jesus referred to as His beloved.

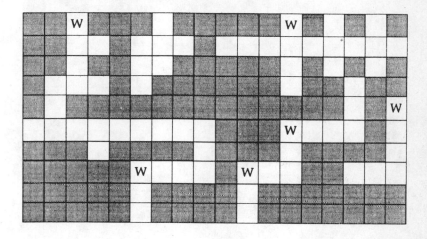

ANSWERS

The verses are John 1:1-2 and here is how they might fit
into the puzzle:

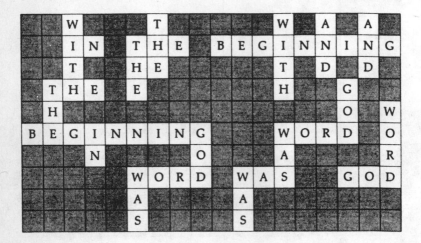

"This is the disciple who testifies to these things and who wrote
them down. We know that his testimony is true. Jesus did many
other things as well. If every one of them were written down, I
suppose that even the whole world would not have room for the
books that would be written." John 21:24-25

The last two verses of John, in case you were wondering.

CAMP RULES FOR THE HEBREW

*There are some things you just shouldn't have
to tell a person.*

Don't take advantage of orphans or widows. Exodus 22:22

Don't follow the crowd. Exodus 23:2

Every year, have three great big parties. Exodus 23:14

If you buy a Hebrew servant, you have to let him go after six years. Exodus 21:2

If a man marries more than one women, he can't deny the first wife food, clothes, and marital rights. Exodus 21:10

Don't eat animals that chew cud. Rabbits and camels, for example. Leviticus 11:4-5

Don't eat blood. Or is it drink blood? Leviticus 17:14

Don't cut yourself on purpose. Leviticus 19:28

Stand up around the elderly. Leviticus 19:32

Don't offer an animal with warts as an offering.
Leviticus 22:22

Remember the story of Uzzah who died because he touched the ark of the covenant? The event made David angry with God, so he named the place Perez-Uzzah.
1 Chronicles 13:11

Rehoboam, Solomon's son, had 28 sons and 60 daughters.
2 Chronicles 11:21

The Israelites couldn't eat storks.
Leviticus 11:19

Some people, including Herod, thought that Jesus was John the Baptist raised from the dead. Mark 6:14

Some other people, thought He was Elijah. Mark 6:15

God made Adam and Eve's first clothes, aside from the fig leaves, of course. Genesis 3:21

God allowed Israel to drive out other nations from Canaan because those nations were evil, not because Israel was so righteous. Deuteronomy 9:4-5

During the Passover, Israelites couldn't break any of the bones in their feast, not even the wishbone. Exodus 12:46

Jesus chose 72 people to travel by twos ahead of him and to heal people. Luke 10:10

WHO AM I?

1. I lived in Antioch and predicted a severe famine that affected the entire Roman world.

2. I died when Joab stabbed me in the stomach. I miss being the commander of Saul's army.

3. Because I was the god of Ekron, Ahaziah tried to consult me about a certain injury.

4. My husband Felix and I listened to Paul talk about Jesus while he was on trial.

5. After I died, my widow Naomi and our devoted daughter-in-law had to begin a new life.

6. I gave my friend David my clothes, my sword, my bow, and my belt.

7. As an archangel, I argued with the devil over Moses' body.

8. My king, David, forced me into a disastrous battle, and when I was killed he married my wife.

9. My useless husband replaced me as queen with a Jewish girl.

10. As king of Moab, I tried to hire Balaam to curse Israel.

ANSWERS

1. Agabus. Acts 11:28

2. Abner. 2 Samuel 3:27

3. Baal-Zebub. 2 Kings 1:2

4. Drusilla. Acts 24:24

5. Elimelech. Ruth 1:3

6. Jonathan. 1 Samuel 18:4

7. Michael. Jude 9

8. Uriah. 2 Samuel 11:15

9. Vashti. Esther 2:1-4

10. Balak. Numbers 22:24

WHERE'S THE VERSE?

You know it's in there somewhere, don't you.

1. "I am the resurrection and the life. He who believes in me will live even though he dies."

2. "Here I am. I stand at the door and knock."

3. "That if you confess with your mouth, 'Jesus is Lord,' and believe in your heart that God raised Him from the dead, you will be saved."

4. "For this reason a man will leave his father and mother and be united to his wife, and they will become one flesh."

5. "Our Father in heaven, hallowed be your name."

6. "A record of the genealogy of Jesus Christ the son of David, the son of Abraham:. . ."

7. "For as lightning that comes from the east is visible even in the west, so will be the coming of the Son of Man."

8. "It is easier for a camel to go through the eye of a needle than for a rich man to enter the kingdom of Heaven."

9. "Let him kiss me with the kisses of his mouth—for your love is more delightful than wine."

10. "Everyone must submit himself to the governing authorities, for there is no authority except that which God has established."

ANSWERS

1. John 11:25

2. Revelation 3:20

3. Romans 10:9

4. Genesis 2:24

5. Matthew 6:9

6. Matthew 1:1

7. Matthew 24:27

8. Matthew 9:23

9. Song of Songs 1:2

10. Romans 13:1

Once when Paul and Silas were in prison,
an earthquake shook the doors open.
Acts 16:26

Jesus means "the Lord saves."

When Aaron and his sons were ordained, Moses had to put ram's blood on their right ear lobes, right thumbs, and right big toes. Exodus 29:20

Priscilla and Aquila moved to Corinth because Claudius, the emperor, made all the Jews leave Rome. Acts 18:2

All the tribes of Israel got part of the promised land except the Levites. Numbers 26:62

Jesus once made some demons keep quiet after He drove them out because they knew who He was, and He wanted to keep His identity to himself for awhile. Mark 1:34

People with running sores couldn't present offerings to God. Leviticus 21:18

If an Israelite wanted to marry a captive woman, he had to make her shave her head, trim her nails, and change her clothes. So much for the lovely bride.
Deuteronomy 21:12-13

Whenever evil spirits saw Jesus, they fell down and yelled, "You are the Son of God." Mark 3:11

FOUR-THINGS

There were too many to fit on one page

Zacchaeus paid back the people he cheated four times over.
Luke 19:8

Peter was arrested by four squads of four soldiers each.
Acts 12:4

Philip had four prophesying daughters. Acts 21:9

John saw four creatures in front of the throne, and they
were covered with eyes. Revelation 4:6

Lazarus was in his tomb for four days. John 11:37

After Jesus was crucified, the soldiers divided up His
clothes into four shares. John 19:23

Zechariah saw four chariots, four craftsman, and four
horses. Zechariah 1:18, 20, 6:1

Daniel saw four winds of heaven and four beasts, at least
one with four wings and four heads. Daniel 7:3-6

Solomon's Quandry

That Solomon, what a guy! Finish his thoughts from Proverbs 30 on the things that perplexed him.

1. "Four things on earth are small, yet they are extremely wise." What are they?

2. "There are three things that are never satisfied, four that never say, 'Enough.'" What are they?

3. "There are three things that are too amazing for me, four that I do not understand." What are they?

4. "Under three things the earth trembles, under four it cannot bear up." What are they?

5. "There are three things that are stately in their stride, four that move with stately bearing." What are they?

ANSWERS

1. Ants, coneys, locusts, and lizards. Verses 24-28

2. The grave, a barren womb, land that needs water, and fire. Verses 15-16

3. The eagle, the snake, a ship, and a man with a maiden. Verses 18-20

4. A servant who becomes a king, a fool full of food, an unloved woman who is married, and a maid who displaces her mistress. Verses 21-23

5. The lion, a strutting rooster, a he-goat, and a king with his army. Verses 29-31

Wisdom was made before the world began.
Proverbs 8:23

Z Is for Zebra

and that's not all! Find the biblical names that begin with Z in this wordsearch.

```
A H A I D A B E Z Z Z
B Z Y Z A B B A I E E
I Z O P H A R D P B R
Z E D E K I A H P U U
M C A I H B A A O L B
H H L N A N S R R U B
A A T Z I O J E A N A
P R N A V A A Z H K B
L I H C Z E B E D E E
I A N T M A H T E Z L
Z H Z A C C H A E U S
```

Zaavan   Zephaniah   Zabad
Zerubbabel   Zabbai   Zilpah
Zacchaeus   Zipporah   Zebadiah
Zerah   Zebedee   Zetham
Zebulun   Ziba   Zechariah
        Zophar   Zedekiah

WORDSEARCH SOLUTION

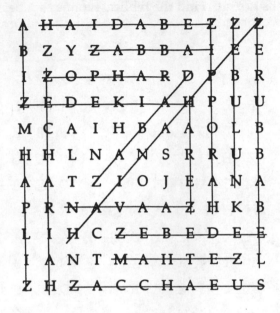

```
A  H  A  I  D  A  B  E  Z  Z  Z
B  Z  Y  Z  A  B  B  A  I  E  E
I  Z  O  P  H  A  R  D  P  B  R
Z  E  D  E  K  I  A  H  P  U  U
M  C  A  I  H  B  A  A  O  L  B
H  H  L  N  A  N  S  R  R  U  B
A  A  T  Z  I  O  J  E  A  N  A
P  R  N  A  V  A  A  Z  H  K  B
L  I  H  C  Z  E  B  E  D  E  E
I  A  N  T  M  A  H  T  E  Z  L
Z  H  Z  A  C  C  H  A  E  U  S
```

HOOK, LINE, AND SOLDIER

Under David's rule, there were more than one million men who could handle a sword in Israel. 1 Chronicles 21:5

Solomon built the temple on Mount Moriah.
2 Chronicles 3:1

Ham, Noah's son, was the father of Canaan. Genesis 11:22

? Where was Paul when he had his hair cut off?
Cenchrea. Acts 18:18

When the Assyrians took Manasseh prisoner, they put a hook in his nose. 2 Chronicles 33:11

Jochebed, Moses' mother, married Amram, Moses' father, who was her nephew. Does that make Moses and Amram cousins, or what? Exodus 6:20

After Jesus was resurrected, He ate a piece of boiled fish with His disciples. Luke 24:42-43

While some priests were carrying the ark of the covenant, the Jordan River dried up so they could cross on dry ground. Joshua 3:15-17

EAT, DRINK, AND BE. . .

"Do not get drunk on wine, which leads to debauchery,"
Ephesians 5:18. Here is a list of people who either didn't heed this
timeless advice or were just misunderstood.

Noah. He was definitely not misunderstood. Genesis 9:21

Eli thought Hannah was drunk, but she was just praying quietly. 1 Samuel 1:13

On the day of Pentecost, some people thought the believers had had too much wine. Acts 2:13

Lot, more than once. Genesis 19:33, 35

Jesus was called a drunkard by some of the Pharisees. Matthew 11:19

Nabal, whose wife Abigail saved him from the wrath of David. 1 Samuel 25:36

Uriah got drunk the night before he died in battle, thanks to David. 2 Samuel 11:13

"Drink, get drunk, and vomit."
Jeremiah 25:27

It Happened in the New Testament...Didn't it?

Answer the following True/False questions pertaining to the New Testament.

1. Hezekiah was John the Baptist's father.

2. Tiberius Caesar was ruler when Jesus was born.

3. Jesus made some healing mud by mixing His saliva with dirt.

4. Peter was the disciple "whom Jesus loved."

5. Paul and Barnabas had such a disagreement that they parted company.

6. It was nearly dusk when the Lord caused a bright light to blind Paul.

7. Paul survived a harrowing shipwreck in the Black Sea.

8. Stephen was seized by a disgruntled group called the Synagogue of the Freedmen.

9. Paul had a secretary named Tertius.

10. Mark and Barnabas were brothers.

ANSWERS

1. False. Zechariah was his father. Luke 1:15

2. False. Caesar Augustus was the ruler. Luke 2:1

3. True. John 9:6

4. False. John is believed to be the one. John 13:23

5. True. Acts 15:39

6. False. It was about noon. Acts 22:6

7. False. It is never recorded that he was in the Black Sea.

8. True. Acts 6:9-12

9. True. Romans. 16: 22

10. False. They were cousins. Colossians 4:10

BLESS ME, PLEASE

To which of his many sons was Jacob referring when he handed out these blessings. (Genesis 49)

1. ". . .is a fruitful vine whose branches climb over a wall."

2. "Cursed be their anger, so fierce, and their fury, so cruel!"

3. ". . .will be a serpent by the roadside, a viper along the path."

4. " He will live by the seashore."

5. ". . .he will bend his shoulder to the burden and submit to forced labor."

6. "You are my firstborn, my might, the first sign of my strength."

7. ". . .will be attacked by a band of raiders."

8. "He will tether his donkey to a vine, his colt to the choicest branch."

9. "His food will be rich."

10. "He is a doe set free that bears beautiful fawns."

11. "He devours his prey in the morning and divides the plunder at night."

ANSWERS

1. Joseph.

2. Simeon and Levi.

3. Dan.

4. Zebulun.

5. Issachar.

6. Reuben.

7. Gad.

8. Judah.

9. Asher.

10. Naphtali.

11. Benjamin.

Ah, Man's Best Friend

Dogs didn't bark at the Israelites during the plague on the firstborn in Egypt. Exodus 11:7

Dogs ate those belonging to Jeroboam. 1 Kings 14:11

Dogs ate those belonging to Baasha. 1 Kings 16:4

And, dogs ate those belonging to Ahab. 1 Kings 21:24

In fact, dogs licked up Ahab's blood. 1 Kings 22:38

Dogs ate Jezebel, except for her hands and feet.
2 Kings 9:33-36

"Anyone who is among the living has hope—even
a live dog is better off than a dead lion!"
Ecclesiastes 9:4

When Philip met the Ethiopian eunuch, the eunuch was reading Isaiah 53:7-8. Acts 8:32-33

God didn't allow David to build a house for Him because he had caused too much death. Solomon got to do it instead. 1 Chronicles 22:8-10

Once when Peter was really hungry, he saw a sheet full of animals in a vision, and God told him to eat up.
Acts 10:10-13

When Uzziah, an unfaithful king, tried to burn incense to the Lord, leprosy broke out on his forehead.
2 Chronicles 26:19

? Who said, "Why do you spend the night by the wall? If you do this again, I will lay hands on you."

Nehemiah. Nehemiah 13:20

If the disciples had paid for the food to feed the 5,000-plus people, it would have cost eight months' pay. Mark 6:37

Jericho is the "city of palms." 2 Chronicles 28:15

Remember the stone Jacob used as a pillow the night he dreamed about angels? He used the same stone as a pillar to mark the spot. Genesis 28:18

LIKE, A VALLEY QUIZ, YA KNOW

1. The Lord will bring judgment in the Valley of _____.

2. The Valley of Ben Hinnom will become known as the Valley of _____.

3. David killed 18,000 Edomites in the Valley of _____.

4. When people of Sodom and Gomorrah ran from enemy kings, they got stuck in tar pits in the Valley of _____.

5. The 12 spies of Israel got a huge cluster of grapes from the Valley of _____.

6. Achan was stoned and his body was covered with rocks in the Valley of _____.

7. It was in the Valley of _____ that Gideon tested the Lord with a fleece.

8. In the _____ Valley, King Asa burned his grandmother's asherah pole.

9. "Even though I walk through the valley of the _____ _____ _____, I will fear no evil."

ANSWERS

1. Jehoshophat. Joel 3:12

2. Slaughter. Jeremiah 7:32

3. Salt. 2 Samuel 8:13

4. Siddim. Genesis 14:3

5. Eshcol. Numbers 13:23

6. Achor. Joshua 7:26

7. Jezreel. Judges 6:33-40

8. Kidron. 2 Chronicles 15:16

9. Shadow of death. Psalm 23:4

HE WHO HAS EARS
LET HIM HEAR

To whom was Jesus speaking when He said. . .

1. "It is written: 'Man does not live on bread alone, but on every word that comes from the mouth of God.'"

2. "Go! It will be done just as you believed it would."

3. "It is not right to make the children's bread and toss it to their dogs."

4. "Quiet! Be still!"

5. "Get behind me, Satan! You do not have in mind the things of God, but the things of men."

6. "You don't know what you are asking. Can you drink the cup I drink or be baptized with the baptism I am baptized with?"

7. "Go, show yourselves to the priests."

8. "Dear woman, why do you involve me? My time has not yet come"

9. "Go, call your husband and come back."

10. "Your brother will rise again."

ANSWERS

1. Satan. Matthew 4:4

2. The centurion. Matthew 8:13

3. A Canaanite woman. Matthew 15:26

4. The wind and the waves. Mark 4:39

5. Peter. Mark 8:33

6. James and John. Mark 10:38

7. The ten healed lepers. Luke 17:14

8. Mary. John 2:4

9. The Samaritan woman who actually had five husbands. John 4:16

10. Martha. John 11:23

PLENTIFUL POT POURRI

Once, so many people crammed into a house with Jesus that He and His disciples couldn't even eat. Mark 3:20

When the Lord killed the firstborn of Egypt, he even killed the firstborn animals. Exodus 13:15

> **?** Who owned the cattle on 1,000 hills?
> *Asaph. Psalm 50:10*

In order to feed the large crowd of more than 5,000, Jesus organized the people into groups of 100s and 50s.
Mark 6:39-40

While Abimelech governed Israel, he murdered his 70 brothers. Judges 9:5

On the day of Pentecost, a violent wind filled the house where the believers had gathered. Acts 2:2

A woman cracked Abimelech's head with a stone, so he told his armor-bearer to kill him. He didn't want people to say, "a woman killed him." Judges 9:53-54

People used to lay sick people in the streets so that Peter's shadow could heal them as he walked by. Acts 5:15

Definitive Definitions

An ephod is a sleeveless vest worn by priests.

Abba means "dear father" in Aramaic.

Ben, as in Ben-Hadad, means "son" in Hebrew.

Messiah means "anointed one" in Hebrew.

A bier was a bed used for corpses. See 2 Samuel 3:31

Henna, like the blossoms in Song of Songs, is a bush with leaves that are used to color fingernails.

Gall is a bitter extract from a plant in Palestine.

Offal is the waste part of an animal that was burned as an offering.

Old Testament True False

1. When the Israelites left Egypt, they numbered more than 600,000 men, plus women and children.

2. The Passover feast commemorates the day the Israelites were released from Babylon.

3. Tola and Jair were ungodly kings who were defeated by the Midianites as a judgment from God.

4. Samson was from the tribe of Dan.

5. Walleye was the father of Boaz.

6. Gehazi was the name of Elisha's servant.

7. King Zedekiah was the grandson of Jeremiah the prophet.

8. In the last chapter of the Old Testament, Micah wrote about the day of the Lord and the coming of Elijah.

9. Moses killed an Egyptian once and buried his body in the sand.

10. Israelites had trouble conquering Ai because of Achan's sin.

ANSWERS

1. True. Exodus 12:38

2. False. It commemorated their release from Egypt.
   Exodus 12

3. False. They were judges. Judges 10:1-5

4. True. Judges 13:2

5. False. Salmon was his father. Ruth 4:21

6. True. 2 Kings 4:12

7. False. Jeremiah was his grandfather, but not Jeremiah
   the prophet. Jeremiah 52:1

8. False. It was Malachi.

9. True. Exodus 2:12-13

10. True. Joshua 7

WHO SAID. . .

1. "My body is clothed with worms and scabs, my skin is broken and festering."

2. "Ah, the smell of my son is like the smell of a field that the Lord has blessed."

3. "Bless me—me too, my father!"

4. "I'm disgusted with living because of these Hittite women."

5. "You have made a fool of me! If I had a sword in my hand, I would kill you right now."

6. "If there is dew only on the fleece and all the ground is dry, then I will know that you will save Israel by my hand."

7. "What is your servant, that you should notice a dead dog like me?"

8. "This child is destined to cause the falling and rising of many in Israel, and to be a sign that will be spoken against,. . ."

9. "You brood of vipers! Who warned you to flee from the coming wrath?"

10. "I am ready not only to be bound, but also to die in Jerusalem for the name of the Lord Jesus."

ANSWERS

1. Job. Job 7:5

2. Isaac to Jacob. Genesis 27:27

3. Esau to Jacob. Genesis 27:34

4. Rebekah. Genesis 27:46

5. Balaam. Numbers 22:29

6. Gideon. Judges 6:37

7. Mephibosheth. 2 Samuel 9:8

8. Simeon while blessing the baby Jesus. Luke 2:34

9. John the Baptist. Luke 3:7

10. Paul. Acts 21:13

Hang 'Em High

Haman was hanged for plotting against the Jews.
Esther 7:10

Haman's ten sons were hanged on the same gallows.
Esther 9:19

According to Matthew, Judas hanged himself after
betraying Jesus. Matthew 27:5

Bigthan and Teresh were hanged for plotting against King
Xerxes. Esther 2:23

Absalom was hanged in an oak tree by accident, although
the hanging wasn't actually the cause of his death.
2 Samuel 18:9

Pharoah hanged his chief baker, just like the guy's dream
had warned. Genesis 40:22

Ahithophel, David's counselor, hanged himself after his
plot against David was foiled. 2 Samuel 17:23

You've Got to Hear This

Esther sent clean clothes to Mordecai to replace his sackcloth ensemble, but he wouldn't wear them. Esther 4:4

God doesn't tempt people. James 1:13

When Hezekiah and his people were purifying the temple and consecrating the priests, they sacrificed 600 bulls and 3,000 sheep and goats. 2 Chronicles 29:33

In New Testament times, when it was time for a priest to burn incense in the temple, that priest was chosen by casting lots. Luke 1:9

? Who killed Jonathan, Saul's son?

the Philistines. 1 Chronicles 10:2

King Manasseh of Judah was so rotten, he sacrificed his own sons in a fire. 2 Chronicles 33:6

Abram's name was changed to Abraham because Abraham means "father of man," and, well, Abram doesn't.
Genesis 17:5

During the first Passover, the Lord killed even the first born of the livestock in Egypt. Exodus 12:29

SILVER & GOLD

and other shiny things

Choose a precious metal or stone to answer these valuable clues.

1. Abimelech paid a 1,000 shekels of this to vindicate Sarah.

2. Some of the Israelites saw the Lord standing on pavement of this.

3. The magi gave Jesus incense, myrrh, and this for a belated birthday gift.

4. Judas took 30 pieces of this to betray Jesus.

5. During a famine, a donkey's head sold for 80 shekels of this.

6. The good Samaritan gave two coins of this to the innkeeper to help the abused man.

7. There is some of this in Havilah.

8. The Proverbs 31 woman is worth more than this.

9. The 12 gates of heaven are each made a solid one of these.

10. King Nebuchadnezzar made an image of this that was 90 feet high.

ANSWERS

1. Silver. Genesis 20:16

2. Sapphire. Exodus 24:10

3. Gold. Matthew 2:11

4. Silver. Matthew 26:15

5. Silver. 2 Kings 6:25

6. Silver. Luke 10:35

7. Gold. Genesis 2:11

8. Rubies. Proverbs 31:10

9. Pearl. Revelation 21:21

10. Gold. Daniel 3:1

"Be strong and courageous" is written ten times
in the Bible. Take heed.
Deuteronomy 31:3, 6, 7; Joshua 1: 6, 7, 9, 10:25;
1 Chronicles 22:13, 28:20; 2 Chronicles 32:7

AND GOD SAID. . .

To whom was God speaking when He said. . .

1. "Ask for what ever you want me to give you.

2. "Why are you angry? Why is your face downcast?"

3. "Lift up your eyes from where you are and look north and south, east and west."

4. "Reach out your hand and take it by the tail."

5. "Stand up! What are you doing down on your face?"

6. "Rise and anoint him; he is the one."

7. "Very well, then, he is in your hands; but you must spare his life."

8. "Go and buy a linen belt and put it around your waist."

9. "Look, I am setting a plumbline among my people Israel."

10. "Do you have a right to be angry about the vine?"

ANSWERS

1. Solomon. 1 Kings 3:5

2. Cain. Genesis 4:6

3. Abram. Genesis 13:14

4. Moses. Exodus 4:4

5. Joshua. Joshua 7:10

6. Samuel. 1 Samuel 16:12

7. Satan. Job 2:6

8. Jeremiah. Jeremiah 13:1

9. Amos. Amos 7:8

10. Jonah. Jonah 4:9

Wisdom is more valuable than rubies.
Proverbs 8:11

King Josiah purged Judah by burning the priests' bones on their altars. 2 Chronicles 34:5

When Terah and his family left Ur, they were headed for Canaan but settled in Haran instead. Genesis 11:31

Jesus once cursed a fig tree so it wouldn't produce any more figs. Matthew 21:19

After Jacob wrestled with a "man" all night long, his name was changed to Israel. Genesis 32:28

Some people spread a rumor that John the apostle would never die, but it was all a misunderstanding. John 21:23

When Jericho collapsed, the Israelites killed even the animals that were inside the city. Joshua 6:21

When the Egyptians were chasing Moses and the Israelites, God made the wheels fall off of the Egyptians' chariots. Exodus 14:25

Caleb promised his daughter in marriage to the man who conquered an enemy city. His nephew won the prize. Joshua 15:16-17

Adoni-Bezek, a Canaanite, cut off the thumbs and big toes of 70 kings. Judges 1:7

During the flood, water covered the mountains by more than 20 feet. Genesis 7:20

The tabernacle was made with 20 frames on the south side, 20 frames on the north side, 20 posts, 20 bronze bases, and a curtain that was 20 cubits long. Exodus 26:18-27:16

Twenty was the minimum age for serving in the Israelite army. Numbers 1:3

Jacob lived with, and literally worked for, Laban's family for 20 years. Genesis 31:41

Joseph's brothers sold him for 20 shekels of silver. Genesis 37:28

King Jabin of Canaan oppressed the Israelites for 20 years while Deborah was the judge. Judges 4:3

When Moses took a census of the Israelites, everybody 20 years old or older had to pay a ransom for his life. Exodus 30:14

Samson judged Israel for 20 years. Judges 15:20

Love Me Tender

Another Wordsearch

Find the dos and don'ts for love found in 1 Corinthians 13:4-8. When you're finished, gather all the remaining letters, except the Xs, unscramble them, and discover the best part of love.

```
S  X  E  P  R  O  T  E  C  T  S
E  K  N  N  E  S  A  E  V  E  N
L  I  V  E  A  N  H  V  C  R  O
F  N  Y  O  G  T  F  O  X  S  R
S  D  B  R  U  E  I  L  X  T  E
E  U  Y  R  V  J  A  O  X  S  C
E  O  T  O  E  L  I  V  E  U  O
K  R  L  R  U  D  E  E  I  R  R
I  P  L  P  A  T  I  E  N  T  D
N  L  O  V  E  S  H  O  P  E  S
G  P  R  E  S  E  R  V  E  S  X
```

Patient	Kind	Rejoices	Truth
Protects	Trusts	Hopes	Preserves
Envy	Boast	Proud	Rude
Self-seeking	Angry	No records	Evil
	Love (4 times)		

Wordsearch Solution

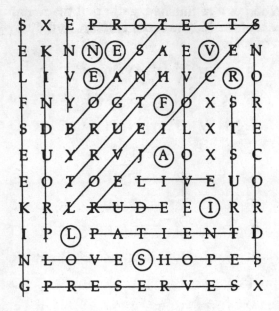

The best part of love;

Love Never Fails

MOUNTAINS

1. Noah's ark rested in the mountains of _____.

2. While Moses was tending his flock near _____, the mountain of God, he saw the burning bush.

3. Moses climbed Mount _____ in Moab and died.

4. Saul and his sons died during a fierce battle on Mount _____.

5. Solomon built a grand temple in Jerusalem on Mount _____.

6. After the Lord had an instructional supper with His disciples, they sang a hymn and went to the Mount of _____.

7. While on Mount _____, Moses took Aaron's priestly garments and gave them to Eleazar.

8. Elijah taunted 450 prophets of Ball during a contest on Mount _____.

9. In the psalm of the Sons of Korah (Psalm 48), Mount _____ is praised as the beautiful city of the Great King.

ANSWERS

1. Ararat. Genesis 8:4

2. Horeb. Exodus 3:1-2

3. Nebo. Exodus 31:1-5

4. Gilboa. 1 Samuel 31:1

5. Moriah. 2 Chronicles 3:1

6. Olives. Matthew 26:30

7. Hor. Numbers 20:27

8. Carmel. 1 Kings 18:27

9. Zion. Psalm 48:2

King Josiah provided from his own livestock 30,000 sheep and goats and 3,000 cows just for one Passover celebration. Eat up! 2 Chronicles 35:7

The Egyptians made slaves out of the Israelites because they were afraid of them. Exodus 1:9-11

Abraham's servant gave Rebekah a nose ring and two bracelets before he asked her family if she could marry Isaac. Boy, what did she get for her birthday? Genesis 24:22

When Jesus walked on the water, His disciples thought he was a ghost. Mark 6:49

? The tree of the knowledge of good and evil was the downfall of Adam and Eve, as we well know. What was the name of the other symbolic tree in Eden?

The Tree of Life Genesis 2:9

Egyptians hated shepherds. Genesis 46:34

Because the priestly garments were so sacred, Hebrew priests had to take a bath before they put them on. Leviticus 16:4

When the early Christians received the Holy Spirit, they were suddenly able to speak in foreign languages. Acts 2:4

WASH THOSE FILTHY HANDS!

The Pharisees criticized the disciples for eating with dirty hands. Mark 7:5

When the men of Judah were taking over Bethel, they spared a man who showed them how to get into the city. Judges 1:24-25

Andrew was a disciple of John the Baptist before he decided to follow Jesus. Wise choice. John 1:35-40

The Mediterranean Sea is also known as the Sea of the Philistines. Exodus 23:31

The Last Supper was a Passover feast. Mark 14:16

Deborah, the judge and prophetess, was married to a man named Lappidoth. Judges 4:4

Moses once sprinkled blood on the Israelites. Exodus 24:8

Joshua and his army won in battle against 31 enemy kings. What a fight! Joshua 12:7-24

Jesus was arrested in an olive grove of all places. John 18:1-3

MYSTERY MAN

Fill in the blanks with a name of a Bible character, unscramble the first letter of each name, and discover who wasn't circumcised until he was 99 years old.

1. _____ was the eunuch assigned to Esther.

2. _____ was one of David's sisters.

3. Aaron's son, _____, was killed for offering unacceptable fire.

4. _____ was one of David's other sisters.

5. This false prophet, _____, was made blind by Paul.

6. Isaac's wife, _____, the one he really wanted, died in childbirth.

7. _____ was the son of Lot's oldest daughter, fathered by lot, incidentally.

Answers

1. *H*athach. Esther 4:5

2. *A*bigail, or Abishai. 1 Chronicles 2:16-17

3. *A*bihu. Leviticus 10

4. *A*bishai, or Abigail. 1 Samuel 26:6

5. *B*ar-Jesus. Acts 13:5-12

6. *R*achel. Genesis 35:18

7. *M*oab. Genesis 19:37

The Mystery Man

Abraham. Genesis 17:24

Oh, the Animal In You

Many people in the Bible were compared to animals. Match these people with their respective beasts or beast parts.

People	Animals
1. Judah	A. Feet of a Deer
2. Issachar	B. Maggot
3. Benjamin	C. Young Stag
4. David	D. Lion's Cub
5. Ishmael	E. Dead Dog
6. The disciples	F. Rawboned Donkey
7. Man	G. Cattle
8. Mephibosheth	H. Ravenous Wolf
9. Job's friends	I. Wild Donkey
10. Solomon	J. Sheep among Wolves

ANSWERS

1. D. Lion's Cub. Genesis 49:9

2. F. Rawboned Donkey. Genesis 49:14

3. H. Ravenous Wolf. Genesis 49:27

4. A. Feet of a Deer. Psalm 18:23

5. I. Wild Donkey. Genesis 16:12

6. J. Sheep among Wolves. Matthew 10:6

7. B. Maggot. Job 25:6

8. E. Dead Dog. 2 Samuel 9:8

9. G. Cattle. Job 18:3

10. C. Young Stag. Song of Songs 2:9

Plant One Right Here

*Here are just a few of the many useful plants
used in the Bible.*

Noah's dove brought an olive leaf back to the ark.
Genesis 8:11

The Israelites used hyssop to smear blood around their
door frames. Exodus 12:22

The temple lampstand was adorned with almond flowers.
Exodus 37:20

Hezekiah's boil was healed by a poultice of figs.
2 Kings 20:7

The Israelites gave a sheaf of the grain they harvested from
their new land as an offering. Leviticus 23:10

Deborah held court in the shade of a palm tree. Judges 4:5

The angel of the Lord spoke to Gideon while sitting under
an oak tree. Judges 6:11

The ostrich lays eggs in the sand and walks away because God didn't give it wisdom. He gave it speed instead. Job 39:13-18

"Is the Lord's arm too short?" That's what God said when Moses doubted His ability to feed the grumbling Hebrews. Numbers 11:22

Jerusalem has a Fish Gate. Nehemiah 3:3

In John's vision, he saw locusts who were told to torture people for five months but not to bother the grass or plants. Revelation 9:2

The Israelites celebrated the harvest for seven days, and during those days they had to live in booths. Leviticus 23:41-43

After Jesus had spent 40 days in the desert being teased by the devil, angels came down and took care of Him. Matthew 4:11

When Mary looked into Jesus' empty tomb, she saw two angels dressed in white and sitting where Jesus had been. John 20:12

It seems that God keeps hail stored up for times of trouble. Heads up! Job 38:22-23

PAUL, A COMPLICATED FELLOW

1. Why did Paul leave Titus in Crete?

2. To whom did he write a letter on behalf of Onesimus?

3. Paul was encouraged when a church remembered him fondly. What church was it?

4. Paul wrote the books of Thessalonians, but what two men were included in his opening lines?

5. Who was the metal worker who caused harm to him?

6. Besides a church organizer, prisoner, and prolific letter writer, what was Paul's other vocation?

7. What was his secret for being content?

8. Complete one of Paul's most well-known commands: "Speak to one another in _____, _____, and _____ _____."

9. Paul once addressed a church by saying "You foolish _____!" Fill in the blank.

10. To what church did Paul give "milk, not solid food."

ANSWERS

1. So he could clean up and appoint elders. Titus 1:5

2. Philemon. Philemon 1

3. The one in Thessalonica. 1 Thessalonians 3:6-7

4. Silas and Timothy.

5. Alexander. 2 Timothy 4:14

6. Tentmaker. Acts 18:3

7. "I can do everything through him who gives me strength." Philippians 4:12-13

8. Psalms, hymns, and spiritual songs. Ephesians 5:19

9. Galations. Galations 3:1

10. The Corinthians. 1 Corinthians 3:2

THE NEW MATH

*"For this very reason, make every effort to
add to your faith. . ."*

According to 2 Peter 1:5-7, what should you add to each of
the following:

1. Faith

2. Perseverance

3. Knowledge

4. Goodness

5. Brotherly kindness

6. Godliness

7. Self-control

PART 2

Fill in the blanks:

"For if you possess these _____ in increasing _____,
they will keep you from being _____ and _____ in your
_____ of our Lord Jesus Christ." 2 Peter 1:8

ANSWERS

1. To faith add goodness

2. To perseverance add godliness

3. To knowledge add self-control

4. To goodness add knowledge

5. The brotherly kindness add love

6. To godliness add brotherly kindness

7. To self-control add perseverance

PART 2

qualities, measure, ineffective,
unproductive, knowledge.

The Thessalonians weren't as noble as the Bereans.
Acts 17:11

God warned Laban in a dream not to say anything to
Laban, good or bad. Genesis 31:24

When the water in Egypt turned into blood, the smell was
so bad nobody could drink it. The smell was the least of
their problems. Exodus 7:31

When Paul was visiting the church in Galatia, he got sick
and had to be taken care of. Galations 4:14

? King Ahab said, "There is still one man through
whom we can inquire of the Lord, but I hate him
because he never prophesies anything good
about me." About whom was he speaking?

Micaiah. 1 Kings 22:8

Once, Abimelech told a story about an olive tree, fig tree,
and a vine who asked a thorn bush to be their king. It said
"yes." Judges 9:8-15

Just like dead flies make perfume stink, so does a little folly
outweigh wisdom and honor, so behave. Ecclesiastes 10:1

Paul wrote with large letters, sometimes. Galatians 6:11

50

The tabernacle curtain had 50 loops and 50 gold clasps.
Exodus 26:5-6

Absalom had 50 men running ahead of his chariot.
2 Samuel 15:1

When Obadiah hid prophets from Jezebel, he split them up into two groups of 50. 1 Kings 18:4

David once paid 50 shekels of silver for a threshing floor and oxen so he could make an offering that would stop a plague. 2 Samuel 24:21-24

The gold nails in the tabernacle weighed 50 shekels.
2 Chronicles 3:9

Because of Elijah's prayer, God sent fire that killed a captain and 50 men, twice. Well, they didn't actually die twice—there were two groups of 50 men each.
2 Kings 1:11-12

Fifty shekels of silver was the price for dedicating a male between 20 and 60 years of age in ancient Hebrew times.
Leviticus 27:3

By Faith. . .

From the eloquent chapter of the book of Hebrews—who did these things by faith?

1. He offered God a better sacrifice than Cain.

2. He obeyed and made his home in the promised land.

3. He gave instructions about his bones.

4. He did not experience death.

5. She welcomed spies and was not killed with her disobedient neighbors.

6. He regarded disgrace for the sake of God to be greater than Egypt's treasures.

7. He condemned the world and became heir of righteousness.

8. He blessed his grandchildren while on his death bed.

9. He blessed his two children in an untraditional order.

10. His parents hid their baby because they saw that he wasn't an ordinary kid.

ANSWERS

1. Abel

2. Abraham

3. Joseph

4. Enoch

5. Rahab

6. Moses

7. Noah

8. Jacob

9. Isaac

10. Moses (Amram and Jochebed)

How the Time Flies

"There is a time for everything, and a season for every activity under heaven." Ecclesiastes 3:1

Make a list of all the activities for which there is a time in Ecclesiastes 3:2-8 and fit them into this puzzle. Hint: The vowels have been left in for your convenience.

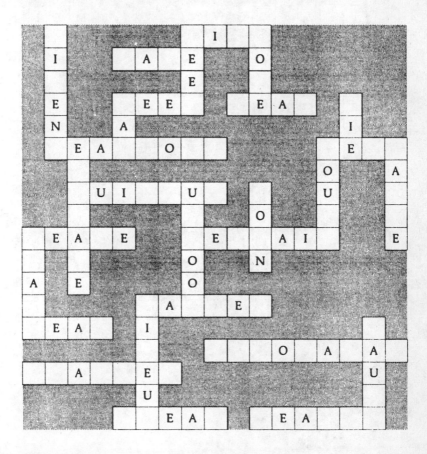

PUZZLE SOLUTION

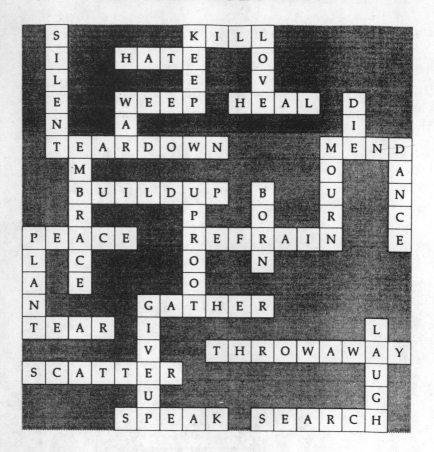

Manna was the "bread of angels." Psalm 78:25

When Jesus returns, His angels will blow trumpets to get everybody together. Matthew 24:31

There was a disabled man who sat at a gate called Beautiful everyday to beg for money, until Peter healed him.
Acts 3:2-7

A fool doesn't know how to get to town. Ecclesiastes 10:15

Even before Jacob and Esau were born, God told Rebekah that the older one would serve the younger one.
Genesis 25:23

After Jesus ascended into heaven, two men in white reassured the disciples that Jesus would come back. Who were those men in white? Acts 1:10-11

The law was given 430 years after God's covenant with Abraham was announced. Galatians 3:16-17

The author of Hebrews thought he had actually written a short letter. Imagine. Hebrews 13:22

When some angels decided to abandon the positions God had assigned to them, God bound them in chains until judgment day. Jude 6

100

Abraham was 100 when Isaac was born. Genesis 21:5

In order to marry Michal, David had to give Saul, her father, 100 Philistine foreskins. 1 Samuel 18:25

In the parable of the seeds, the seed that fell on good soil yielded crops 100 times what was sown. Luke 8:8

The hailstones that fell in John's revealing vision weighed about 100 pounds each. Revelation 16:21

Jacob once bought a camp site for 100 pieces of silver, and it didn't even have hookups. Genesis 33:19

If an Israelite man gave an Israelite woman a bad name, he was fined 100 shekels of silver, and the money went to the girl's father. Deuteronomy 22:19

Elisha once fed 100 men with only 20 loaves of barley bread, and he still had some left over. 2 Kings 4:42-44

A simple rebuke is as effective on a smart person as 100 lashes is on a fool. Proverbs 17:10

TELL ME A STORY

Here is a favorite story of many from Luke 2. Enjoy this little version, and fill in the blanks.

When Caesar _____ was ruler of the _____ world, he issued a _____ that a _____ should be taken.

So, _____ and Mary got on their donkey and traveled to _____ to be counted. Because they couldn't make _____ in those days, all of the inns were _____.

While they were staying in a barn, Mary had a _____. She wrapped him in _____ _____ and put him in a _____.

Meanwhile, some _____ were hanging around the _____ at _____, watching their _____. All of a sudden, an _____ showed up and told them some _____ news—"Today in the town of _____ a _____ has been born to you; he is _____."

Before long, a whole bunch of _____ started singing, "_____ to God in the _____, and on earth _____ to _____ on whom his _____ rests."

After the _____ caught their breath, they went to _____ to see the Christ. When they saw him, they _____ the word about the _____ in the _____.

So, after a hard day, _____ treasured everything in her _____, and the _____ went home _____ God.

The _____

ANSWERS

Paragraph 1: Augustus, Roman, decree, census

Paragraph 2: Joseph, Bethlehem, reservations, full

Paragraph 3: baby, swaddling clothes, manger

Paragraph 4: shepherds, field, night, sheep, angel, good, David, Savior, Christ

Paragraph 5: angels, Glory, highest, peace, men, favor

Paragraph 6: shepherds, Bethlehem, spread, baby, manger

Paragraph 7: Mary, heart, shepherds, praising

Paragraph 8: End

? Who was Jeremiah's secretary?
Baruch. Jeremiah 32:12

WHO KILLED WHO?

1. Abel.

2. The first born of Egypt.

3. Saul.

4. The man of God who spoke with King Jeroboam and was later found dead next to his donkey.

5. Zechariah.

6. An Egyptian who was buried in the sand.

7. Samson.

8. Goliath.

9. Abner, Saul's army commander.

ANSWERS

1. Cain. Genesis 4:8

2. God. Exodus 13:15

3. An Amalekite, because Saul asked him to.
   2 Samuel 1:8; or Saul himself. 1 Samuel 31:4

4. A lion. 1 Kings 13:24

5. The people of Judah by order of Joash.
   2 Chronicles 24:20-22

6. Moses. Exodus 2:12

7. Samson. Judges 16:30

8. David, of course. 1 Samuel 17:50

9. Joab and Abishai. 2 Samuel 3:3

? All hard work brings a profit, but what
does all talk bring?

Poverty. Proverbs 14:23

Pharaoh gave Joseph an Egyptian name—Zaphenath-Paneah. Genesis 41:45

When Mary Magdalene heard someone talk to her at Jesus' tomb, she thought it was the gardner, but it was Jesus instead. John 20:15

A plague once spread through the Israelite camp that killed 24,000 people. Numbers 25:9

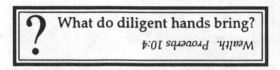

? What do diligent hands bring?
Wealth. Proverbs 10:4

In ancient times, Egyptians wouldn't eat with Hebrews. Genesis 43:32

Noah was the name of one of Zelophehad's daughters, a descendent of Manasseh. Numbers 27:1

Paul's letters were often passed around from church to church. Colossians 4:16

When the Gibeonites were retreating, God threw big hailstones at them and killed more than the Israelites did in battle. Joshua 10:1

LET MY PEOPLE GO, OR ELSE!

Little known facts about the plagues on Egypt

After the frogs that plagued Egypt died, they were put in big piles and made a real stink. Exodus 8:32

The pestering gnats were made from all the dust in Egypt. Exodus 8:17

Moses and Aaron had to take a three-day journey to make a sacrifice to get rid of all the flies. Exodus 8:32

Egyptian magicians turned water into blood, too, so Pharaoh was not impressed with Aaron's "trick." Exodus 7:22

When the Egyptian livestock died, the Israelite animals stayed well. Exodus 9:7

Moses and Aaron gave the Egyptians boils by throwing furnace dust into the air. Exodus 9:10

Before the great hail storm, Moses gave the Egyptians enough time to get their slaves and livestock out of the fields. Exodus 9:19

When God sent darkness, no one could see anyone else for three days. Exodus 10:23

Before Pharaoh let the Israelites go after the last plague, he asked Moses and Aaron to bless him. Exodus 12:32

DYNAMIC DUOS

Who are the familiar, or not so familiar, duos that fit these descriptions?

1. They opposed Moses but their names are not mentioned in the Old Testament.

2. They straightened Paul out on a few things after hearing him speak in the synagogue.

3. These two prayed and sang under adverse circumstances.

4. Paul handed these people over to Satan.

5. The disagreement between these women was worthy of Paul's attention.

6. When everyone else bit their nails and knocked their knees, these two spies kept their courage.

7. These sisters had different priorities when it came to hosting Jesus.

8. These distasteful people proved to be the end of John the Baptist.

9. One was a Tishbite, and the other one was the son of Shaphat.

10. These young fighting men were "one in spirit," and they became friends, despite an antagonistic king.

ANSWERS

1. Jannes and Jambres. 2 Timothy 3:8

2. Priscilla and Aquila. Acts 18:26

3. Paul and Silas. Acts 16:25

4. Himenaeus and Alexander. 1 Timothy 1:20

5. Euodia and Syntche. Philippians 4:23

6. Joshua and Caleb. Numbers 14:6-9

7. Mary and Martha. Luke 10:39-42

8. Herod and Herodius. Matthew 14:6-10

9. Elijah and Elishah. 1 Kings 19:19

10. David and Jonathan. 1 Samuel 18:1

Sing a Little Song

Where can you find these verses that have been turned into hymns or choruses? Where in the Bible, that is?

1. "For you know that it was not with perishable things such as silver or gold that you were redeemed..."

2. "Not by might nor by power, but by my spirit."

3. "Why do the nations conspire and the peoples plot in vain?"

4. "The Lord is my light and my salvation—whom shall I fear?"

5. "This is the day the Lord has made; let us rejoice and be glad in it."

6. "Do you bring in a lamp to put it under a bowl or a bed?"

7. "See, the Lord is coming with thousands upon thousands of his holy ones..."

8. "Now to the King eternal, immortal, invisible, the only God, be honor and glory for ever and ever."

ANSWERS

1. 1 Peter 1:18

2. Zechariah 4:6

3. Psalm 2:1

4. Psalm 27:1

5. Psalm 118:24

6. Mark 4:21

7. Jude 14

8. 1 Timothy 1:17

? Paul planted the seed, Apollos watered it, but who made it grow?

God. 1 Corinthians 3:6

Kings went to war in the spring. 2 Samuel 11:1

Children have angels in heaven who always have an audience with God, so pick on someone your own size.
Matthew 18:10

While David was hiding from Saul, a priest gave him Goliath's sword that had been saved for some reason. It came in handy because David left his at home.
1 Samuel 21:9

Paul was from the tribe of Benjamin. Romans 11:1

? Who said, "I see people; they look like trees walking around."

A blind man who Jesus healed. Mark 8:24

The early church had a list of needy widows, but you had to be over 60, a faithful wife (when you were a wife), and known for good deeds. 1 Timothy 5:9

It was God who hardened Pharaoh's heart so that generation after generation of Israelites would really know that He was the Lord. Exodus 10:1

The saints get to judge the angels. 1 Corinthians 6:3

EVERYONE KNOWS IT'S WINDY

"The wind blows to the south and turns to the north;
round and round it goes." Ecclesiastes 1:6

It was an east wind that brought the locusts to Egypt.
Exodus 10:13

It was a west wind that took them away. Exodus 10:19

God used an east wind to dry up part of the Red Sea.
Exodus 14:21

Isaiah prophesied that God would dry up the Egyptian sea
with a scorching wind. 1 Samuel 11:15

Wind brought quail to the dissatisfied Hebrew people.
Numbers 11:31

A strong wind knocked down Job's house, killing everybody inside. Job 1:19

On one of Paul's trips, the ship he was on was caught in a
"northeaster" for 14 days. Acts 27:14-27

God tormented Jonah with a scorching east wind. Jonah 4:8

Ark, Ark, Who's Got the Ark

1. Who made the ark of the covenant?

2. What tribe did God choose to carry it?

3. What body of water parted when the priests carried the ark into it?

4. After the Hebrews brought the ark from Shiloh, who stole it from them?

5. To whose temple did the enemies take the ark?

6. To what town did the enemies return the ark, along with a guilt offering?

7. In whose house did the Hebrews keep the ark for 20 years?

8. Who kept the ark for David and was blessed because of it?

9. Where did David take the ark, where he kept it in a tent?

10. In what city did Solomon finally put it, in its rightful place—the Most Holy Place?

Answers

1. Bezalel. Exodus 37:1

2. The tribe of Levi. Deuteronomy 10:8

3. The Jordan River. Joshua 3:7

4. The Philistines. 1 Samuel 4:6-11

5. Dagon. 1 Samuel 5:2

6. Beth Shemesh. 1 Samuel 6:13

7. Abinadab. 1 Samuel 7:1-2

8. Obed-Edom. 2 Samuel 6:11

9. Zion, the City of David. 2 Samuel 6:16

10. Jerusalem. 1 Kings 18:1-6

? Who fell off his chair and died when he heard the ark had been stolen?

Eli. 1 Samuel 4:18

OFFER IT UP

In this multiple choice quiz, choose the kind of Old Testament offering that fits the description.

1. This one was given with a gesture.
   A. Burnt   B. Wave   C. Sin

2. This offering was burned outside the camp.
   A. Burnt   B. Guilt   C. Sin

3. Jacob poured this one on a stone pillar.
   A. Drink   B. Fellowship   C. Sin

4. "A pleasing aroma," describes this one.
   A. Drink   B. Burnt   C. Freewill

5. This one consists of flour, along with oil and incense.
   A. Fellowship   B. Grain   C. Guilt

6. Sometimes, this is prepared on a griddle.
   A. Burnt   B. Wave   C. Grain

7. This offering is burned as food, and includes fat from the internal organs.
   A. Freewill   B. Fellowship   C. Sin

8. If someone couldn't afford a lamb, he or she could offer two doves or pigeons for this offering.
   A. Sin   B. Guilt   C. Burnt

9. This offering is presented by someone who committed a violation unintentionally.
   A. Sin   B. Burnt   C. Guilt

10. This offering was kept burning all night.
    A. Sin   B. Fellowship   C. Burnt

ANSWERS

1. B. Wave. Exodus 29:24

2. C. Sin. Exodus 29:14

3. A. Drink. Genesis 35:14

4. B. Burnt. Exodus 29:18

5. B. Grain. Leviticus 2:1

6. C. Grain. Leviticus 2:5

7. B. Fellowship. Leviticus 3:6-11

8. A. Sin. Leviticus 5:7

9. C. Guilt. Leviticus 5:15

10. C. Burnt. Leviticus 6:9

The priest who offered a burnt offering for someone
got to keep the hide. Leviticus 7:8

While King Elah was drunk at his friend's house, Zimre killed him and became the king of Israel. 1 Kings 16:10

Nothing in Solomon's house was made of silver because it wasn't worth much then. 1 Kings 10:21

The Philistines kept Israel from having blacksmiths because they were afraid they would make weapons.
1 Samuel 13:19

God once presented Himself to Elijah with a whisper, preceeded by a rock-shattering wind, an earthquake, and a fire. Now, that's an entrance. 1 Kings 19:11-12

? Bigthan and Teresh—what king did they plan to assassinate?

Xerxes. Esther 2:21

While Paul's ship was in danger during a storm, an angel told him that everybody on board would be fine, but the ship would be destroyed. Acts 27:22-24

Once when the disciples were on the Sea of Galilee, a storm kicked up. Out of nowhere they saw Jesus walking on the water, and when He climbed into the boat, they were all suddenly at the shore. John 6:21

When Solomon got old, he started worshiping false gods. So much for wisdom. 1 Kings 11:4

A FEW MORE BITS OF MISH

or is it Mash?

Abimelech found out that Sarah, whom he had taken into his house, was married because God warned him in a dream. Genesis 20:3

The Saducees didn't believe in the resurrection of the angels. The Pharisees did. Acts 23:8

Paul was stoned once, but not to death. 2 Corinthians 11:25

Solomon wrote 3,000 proverbs and 1,005 songs.
1 Kings 4:32

> **?** What covered the ark of the covenant whenever the Israelite camp moved?
>
> *The shielding curtain. Numbers 4:5*

When an Israelite stole something, he had to return it with an additional fifth of the value in order to make restitution.
Leviticus 6:5

Noah sent out a dove three times to find land.
Genesis 8:9-12

The wave offering was called that because the Israelites waved it at God. Exodus 29:24